C000133708

Walk in the Light Series

Kosher

Scriptural Insights Reveal That The Food Instructions Apply To All Believers

Todd D. Bennett

Shema Yisrael Publications

Kosher
Scriptural Insights Reveal That The Food Instructions
Apply To All Believers

First printing 2005
Second Printing 2014

For information write: Shema Yisrael Publications, 123 Court Street, Herkimer, New York 13350.

ISBN: 0-9768659-0-4
Library of Congress Control Number: 2005903685

Printed in the United States of America.

Please visit our website for other titles:
www.shemayisrael.net

For information regarding publicity for author
interviews call (866) 866-2211

Kosher

Scriptural Insights Reveal That The Food Instructions Apply To All Believers

"You must therefore make a distinction between clean and unclean animals and between unclean and clean birds. Do not defile yourselves by any animal or bird or anything that moves along the ground - those which I have set apart as unclean for you. You are to be set apart to Me because I, YHWH, am set apart, and I have set you apart from the nations to be My own."
Leviticus (Vayiqra) 20:25-26

TABLE OF CONTENTS

Acknowledgments

I must first and foremost acknowledge my Creator, Redeemer and Savior who opened my eyes and showed me the Light. He never gave up on me even when, at times, it seemed that I gave up on Him. He is ever patient and truly awesome. His blessings, mercies and love endure forever and my gratitude and thanksgiving cannot be fully expressed in words.

Were it not for the patience, prayers, love and support of my beautiful wife Janet, and my extraordinary children Morgan and Shemuel, I would never have been able to accomplish this work. They gave me the freedom to pursue the vision and dreams that my Heavenly Father placed within me, and for that I am so very grateful. I love them all more than they will ever know.

Loving thanks to my father for his faithfulness along with his helpful comments and editing. He tirelessly watched and held things together at the office while I was away traveling, researching, speaking and writing.

Introduction

This book is part of a larger body of educational work called the "Walk in the Light" series. In fact, it is a compilation of various content found throughout the rest of the series, which was written as a result of my search for the truth. Having grown up in a major protestant denomination since I was a small child, I had been steeped in doctrine that often times seemed to contradict the very words contained within the Scriptures. I always considered myself to be a Christian although I never took the time to research the origins of Christianity or to understand exactly what the term Christian meant. I simply grew up believing that Christianity was right and every other religion was wrong or deficient.

Now my beliefs were founded on more than simply blind faith. I had experienced a "living God," my life had been transformed by a loving Redeemer and I had been filled with a powerful Spirit. I knew that I was on the right track. Regrettably, I always felt something was lacking. I was certain that there was something more to this religion called Christianity; not in terms of a different God, but what composed this belief system that I subscribed to, and this label that I wore like a badge.

Throughout my Christian walk I experienced many highs and some lows, but along the way I never felt like I fully understood what my faith was all about. Sure, I knew that "Jesus died on the cross for my sins" and that I needed to believe in my heart and confess with my mouth in order

to "be saved." I "asked Jesus into my heart" when I was a child and sincerely believed in what I had done, but something always felt like it was missing. As I grew older, I found myself progressing through different denominations, each time learning and growing, always adding some pieces to the puzzle, but never seeing the entire picture.

College ministry brought me into contact with the baptism of the Holy Spirit and more charismatic assemblies yet, while these people seemed to practice a more complete faith than those in my previous denominations, many of my original questions remained unanswered and even more questions arose. It seemed that at each new step in my faith I added a new adjective to the already ambiguous label "Christian". I went from being a mere Christian to a Full Gospel, New Testament, Charismatic, Spirit Filled, Born Again Christian; although I could never get away from the lingering uneasiness that something was still missing.

For instance, when I read Matthew 7:21-23, I always felt uneasy. In that Scripture passage most English Bibles indicate that Jesus says: "*Not everyone who says to Me, Lord, Lord, will enter the kingdom of heaven, but he who does the will of My Father Who is in heaven. Many will say to Me on that day, Lord, Lord, have we not prophesied in Your name and driven out demons in Your name and done many mighty works in Your name? And then I will say to them openly (publicly), I never knew you; depart from Me, you who act wickedly [disregarding My commands].*" The Amplified Bible.

This passage of Scripture always bothered me because it sounded an awful lot like the modern day Christian Church, in particular, the charismatic churches which I had been attending where the gifts of the Spirit

were operating. According to the Scripture passage it was not the people who **believed** in the spiritual manifestations that were being rejected, it was those who were **actually doing** them. I would think that this would give every Christian pause for concern.

First of all "in that day" there are **many** people who will be calling Him "Lord." They will also be performing incredible spiritual acts in His Name. Ultimately though, the Messiah will openly and publicly tell them to depart from Him. He will tell them that He never knew them and specifically He defines them by their actions, which is the reason for their rejection; they acted wickedly or lawlessly. In short, they disobeyed His commandments. Also, it seems very possible that while they thought they were doing these things in His Name, they were not, because they may have never known His Name. In essence, they did not know Him and He did not know them.

I think that many Christians are haunted by this Scripture because they do not understand who it applies to or what it means and if they were truly honest they must admit that there is no other group on the face of the planet that it can refer to except for the "Christian Church." This series provides the answer to that question and should provide resolution for any who have suffered anxiety over this verse.

Ultimately, my search for answers brought me right back to the starting point of my faith. I was left with the question: "What is the origin and substance of this religion called Christianity?" I was forced to examine the very foundations of my faith and to examine many of the beliefs that I subscribed to and test them against the truth of the Scriptures.

What I found out was nothing short of earth

shattering. I experienced a parapettio, which is a moment in Greek tragedies where the hero realizes that everything he knew was wrong. I discovered that many of the foundations of my faith were not rocks of truth, but rather the sands of lies, deception, corruption and paganism. I saw the Scripture in Jeremiah come true right before my eyes. In many translations, this passage reads: "*O LORD, my strength and my fortress, My refuge in the day of affliction, The Gentiles shall come to You from the ends of the earth and say, "Surely our fathers have inherited lies, worthlessness and unprofitable things. Will a man make gods for himself, which are not gods?"* Jeremiah 16:19-20 NKJV

I discovered that I had inherited lies and false doctrines from the fathers of my faith. I discovered that the faith that I had been steeped in had made gods that were not gods. I saw very clearly how many could say "Lord, Lord" and not really know the Messiah. I discovered that these lies were not just minor discrepancies but critical errors that could possibly have the effect of keeping me out of the New Jerusalem if I continued to practice them. (Revelation 21:27; 22:15).

While part of the problem stemmed from false doctrines which have crept into the Christian religion, it also had to do with anti-Semitism imbedded throughout the centuries and even translation errors in the very Scriptures that I was basing may beliefs upon. A good example is the next verse from the Prophet Jeremiah (Yirmeyahu) where most translations provide: "*Therefore behold, I will this once cause them to know, I will cause them to know My hand and My might; and they shall know that My Name is the LORD.*" Yirmeyahu 16:21 NKJV.

Could our Heavenly Father really be telling us that His Name is "The LORD"? This is a title, not a name and

by the way, won't many people be crying out "Lord, Lord" and be told that He never knew them? It is obvious that you should know someone's name in order to have a relationship with them. How could you possibly say that you know someone if you do not even know their name? So then we must ask: "What is the Name of our Heavenly Father?" The answer to this seeming mystery lies just beneath the surface of the translated text. In fact, if most people took the time to read the translators notes in the front of their "Bible" they would easily discover the problem.

You see the Name of our Creator is found in the Hebrew Scriptures almost 7,000 times. Long ago a false doctrine was perpetrated regarding speaking the Name. It was determined that the Name either could not, or should not, be pronounced and therefore it was replaced. Thus, over the centuries the Name of the Creator that was given to us so we could know Him and be, not only His children, but also His friends, was suppressed and altered. You will now find people using descriptions, titles and variations to replace the Name. Some examples are: God, Lord, Adonai, Jehovah and Ha Shem ("The Name"). These titles, particularly The LORD, are inserted in place of the actual Name that was given in Hebrew text. What a tragedy and what a mistake!

One of the Ten Commandments, also known as the Ten Words, specifically instructs us not to take the Name of the Creator "in vain" and *"He will not hold him guiltless who takes His Name in vain."* (Exodus 20:7). Most Christians have been taught that this simply warns of using the Name lightly or in the context of swearing or in some other disrespectful manner. This certainly is one aspect of the commandment, but if we look further into the Hebrew

word for vain - שָׁוְא (pronounced shav) we find that it has a deeper meaning in the sense of "desolating, uselessness or naught."

Therefore, we have been warned not only to avoid using the Name lightly or disrespectfully, but also not to bring it to naught, which is exactly what has been done over the centuries. The Name of our Creator, which we have the privilege of calling on and praising, has been suppressed to the point where most people do not even know the Name, let alone use it.

This sounds like a conspiracy of cosmic proportions, and it is. Anyone who believes the Scriptures must understand that there is a battle between good and evil. There is an enemy, ha shatan (the adversary), who understands very well the battle that has been raging since the beginning. He will do anything to distract or destroy those searching for the truth, and he is very good at what he does. As you read this book I hope that you will see how people have been confused and deceived regarding the content and meaning of the Scriptures.

My hope is that every reader has an eye opening experience and is forever changed. I sincerely believe that the truths contained in this book, and the "Walk in the Light Series," are essential to avoid the great deception that is being perpetrated upon those who profess to believe in, and follow the Holy One of Yisrael.

This book, and the entire series, is intended to be read by anyone who is searching for the truth. Depending upon your particular religion, customs and traditions, you may find some of the information offensive, difficult to believe or contrary to the doctrines and teachings which you have read or heard throughout your life. This is to be expected and is perfectly understandable, but please realize

that none of the information is meant to criticize anyone or any faith, but merely to reveal truth.

The information contained in this book had better stir up some things or else there would be no reason to write it in the first place. The ultimate question is whether the contents align with the Scriptures and the will of the Creator. My goal is to strip away the layers of tradition that many of us have inherited, and get to the core of the faith that is described in the Scriptures. Part of that involves shedding new light on the dietary instructions.

This book should challenge your thinking and your beliefs and hopefully aid you on your search for truth. May you be blessed in your journey of faith as you endeavor to Walk in the Light.

I

In The Beginning

The title of this book may seem foreign to most people outside of Judaism and word "kosher" (כשר) is something generally misunderstood by anyone who is not "Jewish". The word kosher is a Hebrew word and simply means "to be straight, fit, proper or right; to be acceptable". It is generally used to determine whether something is ritually acceptable.

The most common application of the word in modern times concerns food and the term kosher is often used to describe food that may properly be eaten according to the dietary instructions found within the Torah (תורה).

The Torah is a strange word to anyone outside of Judaism. Christians who read their English Bibles never come across the word in their texts. Instead, they will read "The Law," whenever the word Torah is referenced in the Hebrew Scriptures. Torah actually means "instructions" and it contains instructions from the Creator regarding how to live your life, including what you eat. It is essentially an instruction manual from the Creator for mankind.

Therefore, a person might ask "Is it kosher?" when referring to a particular food. Their question would simply be intended to discern whether something is fit to consume

according to the Torah.

The Scriptural dietary instructions are typically considered to be something exclusively applicable to the "Jews,"[1] but this is simply not true. The dietary instructions were given by the Creator, Whose Hebrew Name is YHWH (יהוה).[2] They are applicable to all mankind, particularly to anyone who desires to follow and obey YHWH. That fact will be clearly demonstrated through this discussion.

Kashrut (כשרות) is a Hebrew word that specifically refers to the dietary instructions found in the Scriptures, although in Rabbinic Judaism it often includes extra-Scriptural regulations.[3] You may be familiar with certain symbols on packaging. Each may have individual meanings within their particular category of kashrut, but all are basically intended to inform the purchaser that the item meets the rigid guidelines established to insure that the product is fit for consumption.[4]

Kashrut is a variation of the word kosher and both terms may be used interchangeably in this discussion to refer to the Scriptural dietary instructions. The reader should keep in mind that whenever either of these terms are used,  they only refer to dietary commandments found within the Torah, not in the Mishnah,[5] The Talmud,[6] the Midrash[7] or other rabbinic writings, unless otherwise indicated.

The reason why most people believe that only "Jews" must be concerned with kosher issues is because they mistakenly believe that the Torah was given only to "Jews" at Mt. Sinai and because they possess a unique position in the eyes of YHWH which makes a majority of the Scriptural commandments applicable only to them.

This thinking is flawed on many levels. Primarily, the notion that YHWH first established regulations concerning food with the "Jews" or rather Yisrael,[8] at Mt. Sinai is not supported by the Scriptures.

From the beginning of creation YHWH gave His commandments to mankind and to the animals concerning the food which they were permitted to eat. To Adam Elohim[9] said, "*29 See, I have given you every plant that yields seed which is on the face of all the earth, and every tree whose fruit yields seed, to you it is for food. 30 And to every beast of the earth, and to every bird of the heavens, and to every creeping creature on the earth, in which there is life, every green plant is for food.*" Genesis (Beresheet) 1:29-30. So we see that in the beginning YHWH regulated the food which was consumed by both man and animals and man's diet was directly correlated with his obedience to YHWH.

While in the garden, Adam did not eat any animals and life in Eden was far different than life as we now know it. Animals were subject to man and all of creation lived together in peace until man violated a commandment of YHWH. The very first recorded transgression of YHWH's commandments was a violation of His dietary instructions: the man and woman ate what they were told was forbidden. (Romans 5:14). This is a transgression which is repeated daily by untold billions who, either intentionally or in ignorance, have decided that they are going to eat whatever they desire whether or not it conflicts with the instructions provided by YHWH. As a result of their disobedience Adam and his wife were cast out of their earthly paradise.

After the fall of man and the eviction from the Garden, the lifestyle of mankind changed drastically. No longer was food provided by YHWH, men thereafter were required to toil for their provisions. According to an ancient text which offers an interesting narration of the expulsion, when Adam and Eve (Hawah):[10]  "were driven out from paradise, they made themselves a booth, and spent seven days mourning and lamenting in great grief. But after seven days, they began to be hungry and started to look for victual to eat and they found it not. Then Hawah said to Adam: 'My master, I am hungry. Go, look for (something) for us to eat. Perchance YHWH Elohim will look back and pity us and recall us to the place which we were before. I and Adam arose and walked seven days over all the land, and found no such victual such as they used to have in paradise. ... And they walked about and searched for nine days, and they found none such as they were used to have in paradise, but found only animal's food. And Adam said to Hawah: 'This hath YHWH provided for animals and brutes to eat; but we must have angels' food ... and YHWH sent divers seeds by Michael the archangel and gave to Adam and showed him how to work and till the ground, that they might have fruit by which they and all their generations might live.'"[11] While the *Vita Adae Et Evae* is certainly not considered to be "canonized"[12] Scripture, it does provide an interesting version of events which is consistent with what we see in recognized Scripture.

There is no record that Adam, Hawah or any of their children ever ate meat after the expulsion from the Garden, although they certainly did offer animal slaughter offerings to YHWH. This is important because one of the significant aspects of the dietary instructions found within

the Torah[13] involves understanding the difference between "clean" (טהרה - tahor) and "unclean" (טמא - tamei) animals.

This distinction was known long before YHWH gave the Torah to Yisrael and was most likely shown to Adam by YHWH when dealing with offerings. This information surely would have then been passed on to Adam's descendents. In fact, the first recorded slaughter offering presented by a man in the Scriptures describes Abel (Hebel) offering the first-born of his flock of sheep, which are considered clean animals. This offering was recorded as being acceptable to YHWH. (Genesis (Beresheet) 4:4).

Generations later, when YHWH called Noah into the ark, He said "*² You shall take with you **seven each of every clean animal**, a male and his female; **two each of animals that are unclean**, a male and his female; ³ also **seven each of birds of the air**, male and female, to keep the species alive on the face of all the earth.⁴ For after seven more days I will cause it to rain on the earth forty days and forty nights, and I will destroy from the face of the earth all living things that I have made." ⁵ And Noah did according to all that YHWH commanded him.⁶ Noah was six hundred years old when the floodwaters were on the earth. ⁷ So Noah, with his sons, his wife, and his sons' wives, went into the ark because of the waters of the flood.⁸ Of clean animals, of animals that are unclean, of birds, and of everything that creeps on the earth, ⁹ two by two they went into the ark to Noah, male and female, as Elohim had commanded Noah."* Genesis (Beresheet) 7:2-9.

Noah was considered "*righteous before YHWH in his generation.*" Genesis (Beresheet) 7:1. As a result, it is safe to say that he observed kosher eating habits. Notice that he took seven of every clean animal and only two of unclean

animals. This is contrary to what I learned in Sunday School regarding the animals herding into the ark. Through pictures, story books and songs, I was raised believing that all of the animals of the world entered the ark "two by two." By misrepresenting the Scriptures, people actually negate the Torah and the Scriptural dietary rules by ignoring and suppressing the truth. If I was provided an accurate picture of what really happened before the flood, I may have recognized the importance of distinguishing between clean and unclean at an early age - a distinction that is vital to those who desire the Way of YHWH.

While in the Ark, Noah did not eat flesh but rather the same food that the animals ate. *"And you shall take for yourself of all food that is eaten, and you shall gather it to yourself; and it shall be food for you and for them."* Genesis (Beresheet) 6:21 NKJV. When the floodwaters receded the Scriptures clearly reveal that he slaughtered only clean animals to YHWH. *"Then Noah built an*  *altar to YHWH and, taking some of all the clean animals and clean birds, he slaughtered burnt offerings on it."* Beresheet 8:21. He was then told: *"³ Every moving creature that lives is food for you. I have given you all, as I gave the green plants. ⁴ But do not eat flesh with its blood."* Beresheet 9:3-4.

This is the first time that YHWH permitted man to eat flesh and there is an implicit understanding that this meant clean flesh and not unclean flesh. This is primarily due to the fact that we were already told that Noah knew the difference between clean and unclean animals. Also, if he ate or slaughtered any of the unclean animals, that would have led to their extinction. On the other hand, he

brought seven pairs of clean animals, which means that there were enough to slaughter, eat and propagate their species.

It is also important to realize that the unclean mammals were generally the predators that ate clean animals. Since the purpose of bringing the animals on the Ark was for them to live, it would not make much sense if Noah were to eat unclean animals and bring about their extinction after saving them from the floodwaters. (Beresheet 6:19-20).

The commandment concerning meat is actually quite profound because it demonstrates the great changes in the planet that resulted from iniquity - the transgression of the commandments of YHWH. You see the purpose of creation was to establish a paradise where both man and beast existed in perfect harmony with each other and with YHWH. Creation was designed so that both man and beast could live off the fruit of the earth.

The persistent and continuous transgression of the commandments brought about judgment and creation slipped further and further from the perfect order intended by YHWH. The entire environmental ecosystem of the earth changed when the firmament from the sky fell to the earth and the water from the depths flowed from below causing the flood. (Beresheet 7:11).

Prior to the flood there were large amounts of water under the earth as well as a great layer of water above the earth that formed a very healthy environment, blocking dangerous ultraviolet rays and producing a very moist, humid, tropical like setting. It was the collapse of this layer that allowed so much water to fall to the earth and flood the planet.

That firmament no longer exists above the planet and there is currently not enough water above the earth to cause such a planetary flood. The existence of the firmament meant that atmospheric pressures were different and the oxygen levels were also higher. All of these climatic factors allowed men and animals to live longer and they also grew larger, thus providing an ideal environment for dinosaurs and giants. (Beresheet 6:4).

The planet had different light that would have diffused through the firmament, and even sound may have been different. Some scientists speculate that light may have even resonated sounds and that the stars emitted music.[14] This is confirmed in the Book of Job which states: *"4 Where were you when I laid the foundations of the earth? Tell Me, if you have understanding. 5 Who determined its measurements? Surely you know! Or who stretched the line upon it? 6 To what were its foundations fastened? Or who laid its cornerstone, 7 When the morning stars sang together, and all the sons of [Elohim] shouted for joy?"* Job 38:4-7 NKJV.

Needless to say, life on planet earth would have been very different before the flood. Immediately after the flood, all of the vegetation would have been destroyed and Noah would have been unable to carry enough food to hold over for an entire growing season. Also, all fresh fruits and vegetables would have perished by the end of the flood.

While the dove returning to the ark with a shoot from an olive tree would have meant that some vegetation had begun sprouting (Beresheet 8:11), the olive tree is an

extremely hearty tree that can overcome tremendous hardship to survive. The olive tree blossoming was a beautiful symbol provided by YHWH and was an exception rather than the rule. The olive tree, which always represents Yisrael, the set apart assembly of YHWH, sprang forth and survived the judgment of YHWH. This shows us that the Elect of YHWH will remain and live after His judgment.

It appears that as a result of the lack of vegetation after the flood, man needed to kill animals and eat meat to survive. There is speculation that man needed the protein offered by the consumption of flesh due to the extreme atmospheric changes. What is clear is that Elohim now gave Noah and his descendants a right that had never been given to Adam or his progeny - permission to eat meat.

Some sages believe that: "Noah was given the right to eat meat, just as Elohim had given Adam the right to eat vegetation, because (a) Had it not been for the righteousness of Noah, no life would have survived the Flood; and (b) he had toiled over the animals and attended to their needs in the Ark. Of him was it said, '*You shall eat the toil of your hands*' Psalms (Tehillim) 128:2. Thus Noah had acquired rights over them."[15]

This new right to eat flesh resulted in the advent of the nomadic lifestyle that men such as Abraham and his descendents endeavored upon. They wandered to find water and food for their livestock, in other words, they toiled over the animals which they would eventually eat. Interestingly, this seems to be in contrast to those who

became hunters like Nimrod, Esau and arguably Ishmael. (Beresheet 10:9, 25:27, 16:12).

Therefore, after the Flood, the lives of animals "with souls" were killed, and blood was shed to provide sustenance and life for mankind (Beresheet 9:4). This was not the tranquil creation that YHWH had intended and was the direct result of disobedience. Most slaughterings were not merely associated with eating, but were also presented as offerings to  YHWH. Therefore, we can see how the shedding of blood, which resulted in death to the offering, resulted in life to the one presenting the offering: thus setting the precedent for the work of Messiah.

Based upon the foregoing, it is clear that kashrut existed well before there was any such thing as a Hebrew or the nation of Yisrael. Simply because the dietary laws were codified in the Torah does not mean that they were new, or specifically for the "Jews" as is often taught. Rather, it was always YHWH's desire for those who follow Him to know the difference between clean and unclean. It was written down in the Torah because one of the purposes of the Torah was to provide a written code for the commonwealth of Yisrael, a people set apart to YHWH. It is evident that YHWH set forth a standard for righteous living prior to the Torah. It is also reasonable to believe that YHWH has not changed that standard. *"For I am YHWH, I do not change."* Malachi 3:6.

2

The Scriptural Dietary Instructions

When people ask me why I do not eat certain things I simply respond: "Because YHWH says so in the Scriptures." The next question is usually: "Where does He say it?" Before my eyes were opened to this important subject I would not have known the answer to that question which is quite remarkable. Having been a Christian all of my life I prided myself in how many times that I had read the Bible. While I knew that Elohim said something to Yisrael about food, I could not tell you where to find it because I never thought it applied to me. Needless to say, the Torah has a lot to say about this subject. To better understand this topic it is fitting to examine the dietary instructions found within the Torah and then look at their application.

The instructions regarding food are found in Chapter 11 of the Book of Leviticus, more accurately

described as the Scroll of Vayiqra. Instead of condensing them or summarizing the list I felt that it would be appropriate to provide the entire text to take some of the mystery out of the Torah portion.

"*1 Now YHWH spoke to Moses (Mosheh) and Aaron (Aharon), saying to them, 2 Speak to the children of Yisrael, saying, 'These are the animals which you may eat among all the animals that are on the earth:* 3 **Among the animals, whatever divides the hoof, having cloven hooves and chewing the cud - that you may eat.** 4 **Nevertheless these you shall not eat among those that chew the cud or those that have cloven hooves: the camel, because it chews the cud but does not have cloven hooves, is unclean to you;** 5 **the rock badger, because it chews the cud but does not have cloven hooves, is unclean to you;** 6 **the hare, because it chews the cud but does not have cloven hooves, is unclean to you;** 7 **and the swine, though it divides the hoof, having cloven hooves, yet does not chew the cud, is unclean to you.** *Their flesh you shall not eat, and their carcasses you shall not touch. They are unclean to you.* 9 **These you may eat of all that are in the water: whatever in the water has fins and scales, whether in the seas or in the rivers - that you may eat.** 10 *But all in the seas or in the rivers that do not have fins and scales, all that move in the water or any living thing which is in the water, they are an abomination to you.* 11 They shall be an abomination to you; you shall not eat their flesh, but you shall regard their carcasses as an abomination. *12* Whatever in the water does not have fins or scales - that shall be an abomination to you. *13* And these you shall regard as an abomination among the birds; they shall not be eaten, they are an abomination: the eagle, the vulture, the buzzard, *14* the kite, and the falcon after its kind; *15* every raven after its kind, *16* the ostrich, the short-eared owl, the sea gull, and the hawk after its kind; *17* the little owl, the fisher owl, and the screech owl; *18* the white owl, the pelican and the carrion vulture; *19* the stork, the heron after its kind, the hoopoe, and the bat. *20* **All flying insects that creep on all fours shall be an abomination to you. *21* Yet these you may eat of every flying insect that creeps on all fours: those which have jointed legs above their feet with which to leap on the earth.** *22* These you may eat: the locust after its kind, the destroying locust after its kind, the cricket after its kind, and the grasshopper after its kind. *23* But all other flying insects which have four feet shall be an abomination to you. *24* By these you shall become unclean; whoever touches the carcass of any of them shall be unclean until evening; *25* whoever carries part of the carcass of any of them shall wash his clothes and be unclean until evening: *26* The carcass of any animal which divides the foot, but is not cloven-hoofed or does not chew the cud, is unclean to you. Everyone who touches it shall be unclean. *27* **And whatever goes on its**

paws, among all kinds of animals that go on all fours, those are unclean to you. Whoever touches any such carcass shall be unclean until evening. ²⁸ Whoever carries any such carcass shall wash his clothes and be unclean until evening. It is unclean to you. ²⁹ These also shall be unclean to you among the creeping things that creep on the earth: the mole, the mouse, and the large lizard after its kind; ³⁰ the gecko, the monitor lizard, the sand reptile, the sand lizard, and the chameleon. ³¹ These are unclean to you among all that creep. Whoever touches them when they are dead shall be unclean until evening. . . . ⁴¹ And every creeping thing that creeps on the earth shall be an abomination. It shall not be eaten. ⁴² Whatever crawls on its belly, whatever goes on all fours, or whatever has many feet among all creeping things that creep on the earth - these you shall not eat, for they are an abomination. ⁴³ You shall not make yourselves abominable with any creeping thing that creeps; nor shall you make yourselves unclean with them, lest you be defiled by them. ⁴⁴ For I am YHWH your Elohim. You shall therefore consecrate yourselves, and you shall be holy; for I am holy. Neither shall you defile yourselves with any creeping thing that creeps on the earth. ⁴⁵ For I am YHWH who brings you up out of the land of Egypt (Mitsrayim), to be your Elohim. You shall therefore be holy, for I am holy. ⁴⁶ This

is the Torah of the animals and the birds and every living creature that moves in the waters, and of every creature that creeps on the earth, [47] to distinguish between the unclean and the clean, and between the animal that may be eaten and the animal that may not be eaten." Leviticus (Vayiqra) 11:1-32, 41-47.

Notice that the emphasis is on being holy, more accurately described in Hebrew as "qadosh" (קָדוֹשׁ), which means "set apart." YHWH does not want His people doing the same things as the rest of the inhabitants of the world who do not follow Him. He wants His people to be set apart and consecrated unto Him.

Observing the dietary commands is more about being like YHWH than it has to do with the covenant made with Yisrael. In verse 44 YHWH says: *"be set apart as I am set apart"* not "be set apart as the covenant I made with you is set apart." We do not blindly observe the dietary instructions simply because we are commanded to do so under a covenant. Rather, we observe the dietary commandments because we want to be more like YHWH - set apart. It is both an individual mandate and a corporate mandate

YHWH has designated certain animals as unclean, abominable and detestable for eating, just as He has designated certain acts as abominable, detestable and unclean that defile a person. YHWH defines sexual immorality in Vayiqra Chapter 18, and calls all of those acts abominable. I am certain that most people with any degree of morality would agree that the acts listed in Vayiqra Chapter 18 are, in fact, still abominable even though they are found in the Old Testament (Tanak).[16]

Likewise, eating abominable things is still abominable. In fact, YHWH uses the same Hebrew word "tamei" (טמא) when describing the pollution and defilement that results from eating prohibited animals or participating in prohibited sexual acts. All are abominable.

Once again, in the Book (Sefer) of Deuteronomy (Debarim), YHWH's dietary regulations are set forth as follows:

"*² for you are a people holy [set apart] to YHWH your Elohim. Out of all the peoples on the face of the earth, YHWH has chosen you to be his treasured possession. ³ Do not eat any detestable thing.* ⁴ These are the animals you may eat: the ox, the sheep, the goat, ⁵ the deer, the gazelle, the roe deer, the wild goat, the ibex, the antelope and the mountain sheep. ⁶ You may eat any animal that has a split hoof divided in two and that chews the cud. ⁷ However, of those that chew the cud or that have a split hoof completely divided you may not eat the camel, the rabbit or the coney. Although they chew the cud, they do not have a split hoof; they are ceremonially unclean for you. ⁸ **The pig is also unclean; although it has a split hoof, it does not chew the cud. You are not to eat their meat or touch their carcasses.** ⁹ Of all the creatures living in the water, you may eat any that has fins and scales. ¹⁰ But anything that does not have fins and scales you may not eat; for you it is unclean. ¹¹ You may eat any clean bird. ¹² But these you may not eat: the eagle, the vulture, the black vulture, ¹³ the red kite, the black kite, any*

kind of falcon, [14] any kind of raven, [15] the horned owl, the screech owl, the gull, any kind of hawk, [16] the little owl, the great owl, the white owl, [17] the desert owl, the osprey, the cormorant, [18] the stork, any kind of heron, the hoopoe and the bat. [19] All flying insects that swarm are unclean to you; do not eat them. [20] But any winged creature that is clean you may eat. [21] **Do not eat anything you find already dead.** *You may give it to an alien living in any of your towns, and he may eat it, or you may sell it to a foreigner. But you are a people holy to YHWH your Elohim. Do not cook a young goat in its mother's milk.* Debarim 14:2-21.

It is well accepted that when something is repeated in Scriptures, we should take special notice because it is very important. The fact that the dietary instructions were given such an emphasis in the Torah should make anyone give this topic considerable attention. This is particularly true when examining the strong language used by YHWH. Kashrut is not some casual subject that can be lightly disregarded. It demands the study, attention and adherence of anyone committed to obeying YHWH and desiring to be transformed into His image.

In the Book (Sefer) of Vayiqra additional dietary rules were given to Mosheh by YHWH. *"[23] Say to the Yisraelites: 'Do not eat any of the fat of cattle, sheep or goats. [24] The fat of an animal found dead or torn by wild animals may be used for any other purpose, but you must not eat it. [25] Anyone who eats the fat of an animal from which an offering by fire may be made to YHWH must be cut off from his people.'"* Vayiqra 7:23-25.

The fat is known as "chelev" (חלב) and is found on

the flanks and certain internal organs such as the kidneys and intestines. It is also believed that the Torah forbids eating the sciatic nerve, known as the "gid ha'na'sheh," which must be removed from the hind leg before eating. (see Beresheet 32:32).

YHWH also forbids the consumption of blood. *"²⁶ And wherever you live, you must not eat the blood of any bird or animal. ²⁷ If anyone eats blood, that person must be cut off from his people."* Vayiqra 7:26-27. *"¹⁰ And whatever man of the house of Yisrael, or of the strangers who dwell among you, who eats any blood, I will set My face against that person who eats blood, and will cut him off from among his people.¹¹* **For the life of the flesh is in the blood,** *and I have given it to you upon the altar to make atonement for your souls; for it is the blood that makes atonement for the soul.¹² Therefore I said to the children of Yisrael,* **'No one among you shall eat blood, nor shall any stranger who dwells among you eat blood.'"** Vayiqra 17:10-12.

Notice that it was not just native Yisraelites who were to abstain from the blood, but those strangers who were with them. The Torah makes a distinction between the stranger and a member of the assembly. If you want to remain a stranger, then you do not have to obey all of the Torah but if you want to dwell with YHWH as part of the set apart assembly, you have to live a clean life and obey His ordinances. If a Christian or any other person who loves and obeys YHWH desires to be "grafted in"¹⁷ and become part of the set apart assembly, they are no longer strangers, they are adopted sons and daughters of the covenant and therefore need to keep kashrut in order to dwell within the community of faith.

The life is in the blood and the blood must return to YHWH. Just as with some sacrifices, the blood was

sprinkled on the Altar and the fat was burned, but the flesh could be eaten; so with food eaten outside of the House of YHWH (Bais HaMikdash), the flesh may be eaten, but the blood must be poured on the ground. (Debarim 12:15-25). In other words, people were permitted to eat meat that was not presented as a sacrifice, although the same prohibition concerning the consumption of blood remained. Removing the blood from meat is commonly known as "kashering" and is one of the steps that make a clean animal fit to eat.

The following passage of Scripture demonstrates how important it is to keep this commandment. "*³¹ Now they had driven back the Philistines that day from Michmash to Ayalon. So the people were very faint.³² And the people rushed on the spoil, and took sheep, oxen, and calves, and slaughtered them on the ground; and the people ate them with the blood.³³ Then they told Saul, saying, 'Look, the people are transgressing against YHWH by eating with the blood!' So he said, 'You have dealt treacherously; roll a large stone to me this day.'³⁴ Then Saul said, 'Disperse yourselves among the people, and say to them, Bring me here every man's ox and every man's sheep, slaughter them here, and eat; and do not sin against YHWH by eating with the blood.' So every one of the people brought his ox with him that night, and slaughtered it there.³⁵ Then Saul built an altar to YHWH. This was the first altar that he built to YHWH.*" 1 Samuel (Shemuel) 14:31-35. Saul was very distressed that his people would commit such a blatant transgression, which was demonstrated by his words and actions.

Sadly, many people in society do not have this type of sensitivity to the commands of YHWH. They feel that meat tastes better when it is bloody and so they end up violating the commands of YHWH in order to satisfy their palettes. I used to be renowned for cooking my filet mignon perfectly pink and juicy on the inside with a

delicious pepper encrusted exterior. If I really wanted to add some flavor I would wrap it with a nice fat slice of bacon. What I and many others failed to realize is that we were consuming the life of the animal (Vayiqra 17:11) when we ate those bloody steaks. It is a transgression of the commandments.

An interesting point on this subject is the fairly recent discovery of microscopic sub-cellular, seemingly indestructible particles, called "somatids." The word "somatid," aptly named by their discoverer, Professor Gaston Naessens, means "tiny particle." Professor Naessens believed that the somatid is the  smallest unit of life, the precursor to DNA, capable of transforming energy into matter.

These somatids are much smaller than cells, and can remain alive for untold centuries. Thus, while blood may dry up and appear "dead," there is still life within it. So you truly are eating the life of another being when you consume blood which always contains somatids. This could be the cause of many of the health problems that plague this society according to the pleomorphic theory of medicine. That subject will be discussed in a later chapter.

3

The Dietary Instructions and Tradition

The dietary instructions are applicable to anyone that desires to worship and obey YHWH. This fact is confirmed in the Messianic Scriptures.[18] The Jerusalem (Yahrushalayim) Council is a common label for the meeting of early believers described in Chapter 15 of the Book of Acts. This issue is discussed in the Walk in the Light Series book entitled "Law and Grace" as it pertained to the Torah and the Gentile converts.[19] It is very clear that the Council did not  convene to determine if Gentile converts should obey the Torah: that was a given. They met because Pharisaic Believers were advocating circumcision as a prerequisite for salvation.

The Council's response to this issue was to write a letter which was distributed amongst the Gentile converts directing obedience to three immediate aspects of Torah observance including the prohibition against: 1) sexual immorality, 2) eating meat sacrificed to idols, and 3) eating blood and strangled animals. Many believe that the Council

mandated that the Gentile converts **only** obey those three requirements, but this is clearly not true since the Gentile converts were expected to go to the Synagogue (gathering place) each Sabbath to hear and learn the Torah (Acts 15:21).[20] The object was for them to learn the commandments over time since they had not been raised in the ways of the Torah.

The Letter to the Gentiles is often misunderstood because of the language used and due to cultural differences. When most people go to a butcher shop or restaurant they typically do not ask how their meal was killed. The commandment not to eat strangled animals encompassed much more than just the method of killing. It also dealt with the type of flesh eaten because it was common practice to strangle pigs, which are unclean. The prohibition against blood is also a very important aspect of kashrut and it would appear obvious that the Letter to the Gentiles found in Acts 15 supports the fact that new converts were to keep the dietary commands. The letter provided some basic instructions on the way to Torah observance. It did not and could not create any new or reduced set of commandments applicable only to new converts. It was a starting point and the clear expectation was that the convert go regularly to the assembly on the Sabbath day, not Sunday, to hear and learn the rest of the Torah.

This notion is simply unacceptable in mainstream Christianity due to false doctrines and poorly translated Scripture passages. While adherents to Judaism accept the fact that the Torah is still a guide for righteous living, most Christians are offended by the idea that they must obey the Torah. They generally profess that they are not "under the law" and, as a result, they are "free" to eat anything. It is

the same notion as: "If it feels good - do it" with a little twist "If it tastes good – eat it". After all they say: "Jesus declared all food clean".

In fact, the Scriptures do say that "Jesus declared all foods clean" but this particular passage does not provide for the abolition of the dietary instructions as so many believe. Let us take a closer look at the passage in the Gospel according to Mark from the New International Version (NIV) Translation. *"[14] Again Jesus called the crowd to Him and said, 'Listen to Me, everyone, and understand this. [15] Nothing outside a man can make him unclean by going into him. Rather, it is what comes out of a man that makes him unclean.' [17] After He had left the crowd and entered the house, his disciples asked him about this parable. [18] 'Are you so dull?' He asked. 'Don't you see that nothing that enters a man from the outside can make him unclean? [19] For it doesn't go into his heart but into his stomach, and then out of his body.'"* (In saying this, Jesus declared all foods "clean.") Mark 7:14-19 NIV.

Notice the information in parenthesis at the end of this passage of Scripture. The parenthesis means that this statement is not in the original Greek manuscript but rather it was a translator's notation, a very ignorant one at that![21] Jesus (Yahushua)[22] was not declaring all foods clean in this Scripture and He never made that statement.

It is simply astounding that a translator would put such an erroneous notation at the end of a passage where the Messiah specifically asks: "Are you so dull?" It is as if the Messiah is asking that question of the translator. The point of His teaching was that it is the heart that gets defiled, not the body. Eating something unclean does not turn someone into an unclean being. Eating pig does not turn a person into pig. They are still a man or a woman. They do not turn into the unclean animal instead. Their body eventually eliminates the unclean thing.

In this instance, the Pharisees were charging Yahushua's disciples with wrongdoing by not washing their hands before eating. At that time, there existed man-made traditions regarding the ritual washing of hands, none of which were found within the Torah. The subject was the Pharisees elevating their traditions over the commands, not the validity of the dietary instructions. The Pharisees had added to the Torah with their own teachings and Yahushua was telling them that they had better examine their hearts, rather than focusing on their traditions. While the dirt on your hands can be easily washed off with water, the heart can be defiled and it is the heart of a man that concerns YHWH.

This has always been the point as expressed by King David in the Psalms (Tehillim). *"³ Who may ascend the hill of YHWH? Who may stand in his holy place? ⁴ He who has clean hands and a pure heart, who does not lift up his soul to an idol or swear by what is false. ⁵ He will receive blessing from YHWH and vindication from Elohim his Savior. ⁶ Such is the generation of those who seek him, who seek your face, O Elohim of Jacob (Yaakob)."* Tehillim 24:3-6.[23]

Another important point regarding the translator's notation after Mark 7:19 is that the statement is redundant because *all foods are clean*. The Hebrew word for food is "akal" (אכל) and the Hebrew word for eating is also "akal" (אכל). Therefore, something cannot be eaten unless it is food and something can only be considered food if it is kosher - which means that it is clean. If it is not kosher then it is unclean and it is not food, regardless of whether or not unbelievers decide to eat it.

If a Hebrew were to read the statement "Jesus declared all foods clean" they would see that it is

superfluous and actually ridiculous. Is it any wonder that "Jews" have not looked to Yahushua as their Messiah. The Christian religion, by changing His Name, His appearance and misrepresenting His teachings has often obscured the True Hebrew Messiah from the Hebrews by presenting Him with a pagan name, doctrine and appearance. Translators have altered His words in direct contradiction of the commandments (Debarim 4:2) portraying His teachings as being in conflict with the Torah which, of course, the Messiah would never do since He is the Living Torah.[24]

While Christianity has a tradition of nullifying the dietary commandments, Judaism has added extensively to the instructions. A modern example of a tradition contravening or adding to the Torah is that which deals with "pareve" dietary regulations.

Traditional Judaism teaches that foods are separated into three distinct categories: 1) meat (basar); 2) dairy (halav); and 3) pareve - which includes all clean fish, foods that grow in the earth and kosher food products. Pareve products are considered to be neutral and therefore may be eaten with either meat or dairy products, but meat and dairy products are not eaten together. This stems from a misguided interpretation of Debarim 14:21 and Shemoth 23:19 which commands: *"Do not cook a young goat (kid) in its mother's milk."*

The passages of Scripture prohibiting the cooking of a kid in its mother's milk are actually prohibiting a practice used in false religions. "It was a custom of the ancient pagans, when they had gathered in all their fruits, to take a kid and boil it in the milk of its dam, and then, in a magical way, to go about and sprinkle with it all their trees and fields, gardens and orchards thinking by these means to

make them fruitful, that they might bring forth more abundantly in the following year."²⁵ This practice is repulsive and abominable in the eyes of YHWH because it contradicts His natural order. Mother's milk is meant to give life and strength to her offspring. To kill and cook a kid in the very substance that was meant to give life to the growing animal is evil. This is what the command was meant to prevent, not the combination of meat with dairy products.

Regrettably, this tradition is so ingrained within Judaism that it has become as powerful as an actual commandment found in the Torah. I cannot even order my daughter a glass of milk with her chicken sandwich in a kosher restaurant in Jerusalem without getting a polite rebuke. This type of teaching becomes a slippery slope, because it then leads to other rules and regulations regarding using different plates and utensils to avoid mixing the meat and dairy.

Pareve kosher is a very pervasive teaching within Judaism and can lead to incredible efforts in order to obey something which is not commanded in the Torah. It is practiced in a variety of ways depending upon one's specific beliefs or even national origin. It is an excellent example of how men and religious leaders heap traditions and customs upon the shoulders of those who desire to be obedient, making Torah observance into a burden.

To prove that this is nothing more than a man made tradition we need only to look to Abraham, the first Hebrew. After entering into the Covenant with YHWH and after his circumcision, he made a meal for YHWH. The Scriptures record that: *"He took butter and milk and the calf which he had prepared and set it before them under the tree as they ate."* Beresheet 18:8. In this passage we see Abraham

preparing a meal consisting of meat and dairy which was given to YHWH and which YHWH ate. Obviously, neither Abraham nor YHWH kept the pareve kosher tradition of separating meat and dairy.

Therefore, while I believe that kashrut is applicable to all who follow YHWH, regardless of your genetic heritage, you must be careful not to adopt traditions into your Torah observance which are not clearly founded upon Scriptural principles: otherwise you may find yourself falling into bondage.

Another tradition that has led to confusion surrounding kashrut is Glatt Kosher. You may see this phrase on certain foods and both restaurants and hotels may advertise that they are Glatt Kosher. There is a common misconception, even amongst "Jews," that Glatt Kosher means extra kosher and applies to chicken and fish as well as meat.

When I first traveled to Israel I had the impression that Glatt Kosher was something that the ultra-orthodox observed. In reality, Glatt is Yiddish for "smooth," and in the context of kashrut, it stems from Talmudic Law. It means that the lungs of a slaughtered animal are smooth, without any adhesions that could prohibit the animal as treifa. Treif (טרף) refers to anything that is not kosher, and the Talmud refers to various physical defects in an animal which would make it treifa. In its truest sense, Glatt Kosher should only apply to meat, and it has become another tradition that is based upon extra-Scriptural authorities and has lead to confusion.

While pareve and Glatt Kosher are not necessarily found in the Scriptures, they are attempts by men to obey the commandments. Although those attempts may have placed burdens upon people it does not mean that kashrut is

still not expected of those who follow YHWH. It is simply important to discern between traditions of men and the plain meaning of Scriptures.

4

The Writings of Paul

The Apostle Paul (Shaul)[26] spent much of his ministry teaching Torah to the Gentiles and helping them to distinguish between tradition and truth when the two contradicted one another. This is why he  was often accused of teaching against the Torah, because he taught against the law, albeit the law of men, not the Law of YHWH. Throughout the centuries, many false doctrines have developed around some of his teachings and there are a number of quotes from his letters which people extract and use in an attempt to demonstrate that he taught against the dietary instructions. In actuality Shaul never taught against the Torah, and it is simply the failure to understand his writings that results in so much confusion. Therefore, it is necessary to review some of those passages in their proper context to discover their true meaning.

The first passage is found in the book of Romans and reads as follows: "*¹ Accept him whose faith is weak, without passing judgment on **disputable matters**. ² one man's*

faith allows him to eat everything, but another man, whose faith is weak, eats only vegetables. ³ The man who eats everything must not look down on him who does not, and the man who does not eat everything must not condemn the man who does, for Elohim has accepted him." Romans 14:1-3.

Most Christians believe that Shaul was teaching that you can eat everything if you have faith and it is only those with weaker faith that have trouble eating everything. To begin with, Shaul speaks of the issue as a "disputable matter". It is imperative that the reader understand that the issue of clean and unclean is **not** a disputable matter. The dietary commands are clearly presented in the Torah and there is no dispute, for example, as to whether or not you can eat pig. In fact, this passage has nothing to do with abolishing the dietary instructions but rather it concerns clean meat offered to idols and vegetarianism. This fact is made clearer from a different translation that states: *"One indeed believes to eat all food, but he who is weak eats only vegetables."*²⁷ Again, something is only food if it is kosher according to the Torah.

In the Roman culture there was a strong connection between temple sacrifices and the meat market. The meat that was sacrificed to idols was often sold by meat vendors. Therefore, a person would have a hard time discerning if the meat that they were purchasing was involved in a pagan ceremony. I imagine that it was awfully hard to find a kosher deli in Rome.  Therefore, some Believers refrained from eating meat, even though it was clean, because they were uncertain whether it was sacrificed to idols. These people were considered weak because they incorrectly believed that the meat was defiled

and made unclean since it was sacrificed in a pagan temple.

Shaul was writing this letter to pagan converts and he spent considerable time in Romans 14 addressing the issue of eating meat involved in pagan temple practices. He was telling the Romans that whatever YHWH has declared clean in His Torah remains clean and no imaginary god or idol can change what was declared clean into something unclean. If you believe otherwise, then you are giving power to the false god or idol, which it does not possess.

Therefore, Shaul is by no means stating that you can eat unclean meat. When he refers to the man who eats everything, he is referring to a person who eats both meat and vegetables. This is a person who is convinced in his or her own mind that the meat is clean, and it is implicit that the meat that he was referring to would be kosher.

In 1 Corinthians 10:25-31 Shaul states: "*²⁵ Eat anything sold in the meat market without raising questions of conscience, ²⁶ for, 'The earth is YHWH's, and everything in it.' ²⁷ If some unbeliever invites you to a meal and you want to go, eat whatever is put before you without raising questions of conscience. ²⁸ But if anyone says to you, 'This has been offered in sacrifice,' then do not eat it, both for the sake of the man who told you and for conscience' sake- ²⁹ the other man's conscience, I mean, not yours. For why should my freedom be judged by another's conscience? ³⁰ If I take part in the meal with thankfulness, why am I denounced because of something I thank Elohim for? ³¹ So whether you eat or drink or whatever you do, do it all for the glory of Elohim.*" 1 Corinthians 10:25-31.

This sounds like Shaul is telling you that you can go to a pagan's house and eat pork if that happens to be on the menu that night. Absolutely not! The important thing is the question that is being raised in the meat market and in the unbeliever's home: "Was this offered to an idol?" If you do not ask the question, then it does not become and issue. On the other hand, if you do ask the question, then you have raised an issue of conscience. It is the same issue that he wrote about to the Romans and it has nothing to do with whether a Believer can eat unclean animals.

In fact, in the midst of this portion Shaul specifically quotes Tehillim 24, which continues to say: "³ *Who may ascend into the hill of the YHWH? Or who may stand in His holy place?* ⁴ **He who has clean hands and a pure heart, who has not lifted up his soul to an idol, nor sworn deceitfully**". Shaul is quoting the Tanak to remind the reader that they must stay pure and not be polluted by the things of the world. He is reinforcing the dietary commandments, not abrogating them.

Another Scripture passage used to justify eating unclean foods is found in the First Letter to Timothy which states: "¹ *Now the Spirit expressly says that in latter times some will depart from the faith, giving heed to deceiving spirits and doctrines of demons,* ² *speaking lies in hypocrisy, having their own conscience seared with a hot iron,* ³ *forbidding to marry, and commanding to abstain from foods which Elohim created to be received with thanksgiving by those who believe and know the truth.*⁴ **For every creature of Elohim is good, and nothing is to be refused if it is received with thanksgiving;** ⁵ **for it is sanctified by the word of Elohim and prayer.**" 1 Timothy 4:1-5.

The reader may unwittingly interpret this passage to mean that every creature is acceptable for food as long as it is received with thanksgiving and prayer. In other words, just say "The Blessing" over your ham dinner, and the unclean flesh supernaturally becomes clean. With that type of Scriptural exegesis you can even be a cannibal as long as

you say your prayers before mealtime. Obviously, this is a ludicrous interpretation, but most all Christians, through tradition, are led to believe this view.

I spent most of my life believing that the special incantation known as "grace" would purify anything on my plate. I later discovered that the Scriptures actually provide the definition of food. Just because you can put something in your mouth and chew it does not mean it is food. It is not actually considered to be food unless it has been declared fit for consumption by YHWH. Therefore when Shaul refers to "*foods which Elohim created,*" he is referring to kosher items that are clean and therefore considered food.

He was addressing a specific problem that arose. Certain people were commanding others to abstain from foods that Elohim created - foods that were kosher. So then, this verse is speaking against those commandments of men that prohibit eating foods that YHWH declared clean. It is simply stating that if the creature is sanctified by the Word (ie. declared clean in the Torah) and prayer, then it is acceptable for food. The only way that food is sanctified by the Word is if it is declared clean in either Vayiqra 11 or Debarim 14, not some mystical invocation spoken over the meal prior to consumption.

I hope by now that it is clear how Christianity, through mistranslating and misinterpreting certain passages, has developed an entirely unbalanced view of food as opposed to the express teachings found within the Torah. This distinction is aptly reflected by the difference between the traditional "Jewish" prayer before a meal and the Christian "grace" which is said before a meal. The "Jewish" blessing which is said before a meal and which was said by Yahushua[28] goes as follows: "Blessed are you

YHWH our Elohim, King of the Universe, who brings forth bread from the Earth." It is a prayer of thanksgiving and an exaltation of YHWH for His provision.

Christians, on the other hand, say "grace" by asking "God" to "Bless this food to our bodies." They typically make this request whether or not what they are eating is actually food prescribed by YHWH. No one who observes the Torah ever needs to ask YHWH to "bless the food" to their body since the food is already sanctified by the Word and therefore they just need to bless YHWH, not the food. This is just another example of how the doctrine of "grace" is often promoted to contrast with the clear teaching of the Torah. One thing is certain: The Grace of YHWH does not conflict with or contradict His Word. While a person is saved "by grace" (Ephesians 2:8) it does not mean that the Torah has been abolished. In fact, if you believe that you have been saved by grace, then you had better demonstrate that faith by obeying the Torah. (James (Yaakob) 2).

The Book of Colossians contains another statement that is often misunderstood by Christians. In this case the poor translation is responsible for changing the meaning of the passage. First we will look at a popular translation and then we will examine the literal translation from the Greek Text. *"¹⁶ So let no one judge you in food or in drink, or regarding a festival or a new moon or sabbaths, ¹⁷ which are a shadow of things to come, but the <u>substance</u> (is) of Christ."* Colossians 2:16-17 NKJV.

This passage appears to say that we are not to judge others concerning their "Christian liberty". The implication is that the festivals (appointed times), the new moon and the Sabbath are not important anymore, because they are only shadows and the real substance is Christ

(Messiah).[29] That is an erroneous interpretation. The word substance is not a correct translation for the Greek word "soma" (soma) which means "body." Also, the word "is" is not found in the original text and was added by translators to make the passage mean what they wanted it to mean.

The literal interpretation of the passage from the Greek reads as follows: "*[16] Then do not let anyone judge you in eating, or in drinking, or in part of a feast, or the new moon, or of Sabbaths, [17] which is a shadow of things coming, but the body of Messiah.*" Now the meaning is crystal clear. Since all of these matters are a shadow of things to come and are all spiritual in nature, do not let anyone outside the Body of Messiah judge in these matters, because only the Body of Messiah is in a position to properly understand and judge concerning those things.

At the time this letter was written, the Believers in Colosse were living in the midst of a pagan sun god worshipping society. When they began observing the Torah, they set themselves apart from the rest of their society by observing Scriptural commandments and abstaining from pagan practices. So then, this statement from Shaul is meant to encourage them in their Torah observance, not discourage them. He is telling them not to be concerned about the judgments coming from the pagans around them because their Scriptural observances were spiritual shadows only understood by members of the Body of Messiah.

Finally, another portion from Shaul's letters that is used to justify eating unclean meats is found in the First Letter to the Corinthians. In that letter Shaul stated: "*[12] All things are lawful for me, but all things are not helpful. All things are lawful for me, but I will not be brought under the power of any. [13] Foods for the stomach and the stomach for foods, but*

Elohim will destroy both it and them. Now the body is not for sexual immorality but for the Master (Yahushua), and the Master (Yahushua) for the body.[14] And Elohim both raised up the Master (Yahushua) and will also raise us up by His power." 1 Corinthians 6:12-14.

It first must be pointed out that this passage is primarily dealing with sexual immorality and not food. Remember that Shaul, through his letters, is responding to certain issues which had been raised in the Corinthian Assembly of Believers. In particular, the Corinthians were dealing with rampant sexual sins, in fact, there was *"such whoring as is not even named among the gentiles . . ."* (1 Corinthians 5:1). The point that Shaul was trying to make was that even though their sexual actions might be lawful under Corinthian Law, they were not "lawful" according to the Torah.

The reason food gets mentioned is to provide the analogy that just as food is made for the belly, so the body is made for YHWH. The word used for *food* is sometimes translated as *meat*. In either case, they derive from the Greek word "bromate" (βρωματα) which means: "meat that is acceptable for food." Therefore, just as clean meat is made for the belly, our bodies, which were made for YHWH, must remain unpolluted and free from the impurities of whoring.

Shaul was rebuking the Corinthians in their attempt to justify their sexual immorality. He was not declaring the Torah or dietary instructions nullified. In fact, in that very passage he specifically stated: *"Foods for the stomach and the stomach for foods."* By now it should be clear to the reader that the word "food" as used by Shaul, a Torah observant Yisraelite,[30] only included clean meats. It should also be abundantly clear that the dietary laws of YHWH still exist

and apply to all those who desire to follow Him.

5

The Vision of Peter

In order to thoroughly respond to the false doctrine which teaches that the dietary commands were abolished we will look at another passage of Scripture involving a vision given to Peter (Kepha).[31] Kepha's vision in the Book of Acts is often used to teach that the dietary laws were annulled. We will first look at the vision and then the interpretation that clearly shows otherwise.

"*9 The next day, as they went on their journey and drew near the city, Kepha went up on the housetop to pray, about the sixth hour.[10] Then he became very hungry and wanted to eat; but while they made ready, he fell into a trance [11] and saw heaven opened and an object like a great sheet bound at the four corners, descending to him and let down to the earth.[12] In it were all kinds of four-footed animals of the earth, wild beasts, creeping things, and birds of the air.[13] And a voice came to him, 'Rise, Kepha; kill and eat.' [14] But Kepha said, 'Not so, Master!' For I*  *have never eaten anything common or unclean." [15] And a voice spoke to him again the second time, '**What Elohim has*** cleansed you must not call common'. [16] *This was done* **three times.** *And the object was taken up into heaven again."* Acts 10:9-16. Many people pick the last statement and miss the entire point of the passage. They use the passage to try to prove that YHWH has decided to declare all things clean, as if one day He just changed His mind about what is food and what is abominable.

It is important to understand that Cornelius, a Gentile, sent three men to seek out Kepha. All three of them were Gentiles, considered to be unclean by Hebrews. To find out the true meaning of the vision it is important to continue with the passage.

"[17] *Now while Kepha wondered within himself what this vision which he had seen meant,* behold, the men who had been sent from Cornelius had made inquiry for Simon's (Shimon's) house, and stood before the gate. [18] And they called and asked whether Shimon, whose surname was Kepha, was lodging there. [19] While Kepha thought about the vision, the Spirit (Ruach) said to him, 'Behold, **three men are seeking you.** [20] Arise therefore, go down and go with them, doubting nothing; for I have sent them.' [21] Then Kepha went down to the men who had been sent to him from Cornelius, and said, 'Yes, I am he whom you seek. For what reason have you come?' [22] And they said, 'Cornelius the centurion, a just man, one who fears Elohim and has a good reputation among all the nation of the Yahudim, was divinely instructed by a set-apart messenger to summon you to his house, and to hear words from you.' [23] Then he invited them in and lodged them. On the next day Kepha went* away with them, and some brethren from Yaffa accompanied him. ²⁴ And the following day they entered Caesarea. Now Cornelius was waiting for them, and had called together his relatives and close friends.²⁵ As Kepha was coming in, Cornelius met him and fell down at his feet and worshiped him.²⁶ But Kepha lifted him up, saying, 'Stand up; I myself am also a man.' ²⁷ And as he talked with him, he went in and found many who had come together.²⁸ Then he said to them, '**You know how unlawful it is for a Yahudite man to keep company with or go to one of another nation. But Elohim has shown me that I should not call any man common or unclean.**²⁹ Therefore I came without objection as soon as I was sent for. I ask, then, for what reason have you sent for me?'³⁰ So Cornelius said, 'four days ago I was fasting until this hour; and at the Ninth hour I prayed in my house, and behold, a man stood before me in bright clothing, ³¹ and said, 'Cornelius, your prayer has been heard, and your alms are remembered in the sight of Elohim.³² Send therefore to Yaffa and call Shimon here, whose surname is Kepha. He is lodging in the house of Shimon, a tanner, by the sea. When he comes, he will speak to you.' ³³ So I sent to you immediately, and you have done well to come. Now therefore, we are all present before Elohim, to hear all the things commanded you by Elohim.' ³⁴ Then Kepha opened his mouth and said: '**In truth I perceive that Elohim shows no partiality.**³⁵ But in every nation whoever

fears Him and works righteousness is accepted by Him.'" Acts 10:16-35.

Now the vision of Kepha should be clear: It concerned the fact that no man should be called unclean and it had nothing to do with food. In order to understand the significance of this vision it is helpful to understand the Hebrew thinking of the day. If you were a Torah observant Hebrew you most likely did not associate with Gentiles because you lived a set apart life. Many Hebrews considered Gentiles to be unclean because they did not observe the commandments. It was actually common to refer to Gentiles as "dogs". This was not correct thinking and resulted in self righteous attitudes. The belief that keeping the Torah made you better than a Gentile is exactly the type of attitude that Yahushua rebuked during His ministry. Were it not for the vision, Kepha may never have realized that the Good News of the Messiah was also for the Gentiles.

According to Adam Clark's Commentary: "[Kepha] now began to understand the import of the vision which he saw at [Yaffa]. A Gentile is not to be avoided because he is a Gentile; [Elohim] is now taking down the partition wall which separated them from the [Yahudim]."[32]

The partition was not only a spiritual partition, but also an actual physical barricade. On the Temple Mount, there was a wall of

Inscription on the Temple wall warning Gentiles to proceed no further

separation that prohibited Gentiles "on pain of death" from entering into the Courts where only Yisraelites were permitted. This sent a resounding message that Gentiles were unclean and somehow inferior to Yisraelites because they could not approach YHWH as could the Yisraelites. The Nation of Yisrael was supposed to shine as a light and draw the Gentiles to YHWH. Sadly, by the attitudes and actions they were actually pushing them away.

Another important underlying meaning in the vision is hidden unless you are aware of the culture and the

Hebraic origins of the faith. Many of the Greek translations describe in the vision: *"a certain vessel descending unto him, as it had been a great sheet knit at the four corners, and let down to the earth."* Acts 10:11 KJV. An analysis of the Greek text clearly reveals that the "vessel" or "object" being lowered by four corners is a tallit, often referred to as a prayer shawl.

"The Tanak frequently uses the phrase 'four corners' to symbolize the whole world. The Hebrew word כנפות (kanfot – 'corners') is also the same for the 'wings' of the angels which abound on the figures resembling human beings in Ezekiel's vision of the chariot (מעשׂה מרכבה; ma'aseh merkava) (cf. Ezekiel 1; Suk. 28a). The tallit or 'prayer shawl' also has 'four corners [ארבע כנפות]' to which the ציצית (tzit tzit – 'fringes') are affixed."[33]

The tzit tzit (tzitzit) are commanded in the Torah in two separate instances. In Debarim 22:12 YHWH commands: *"Make tzitzit (tassels) on the four corners of the*

garment with which you cover yourself." According to Bemidbar 15:37-41: "*³⁷ YHWH spoke to Moses (Mosheh), saying, ³⁸ Speak to the children of Yisrael, and you shall say to them to make tzitziyot on the corners of their garments throughout their generations, and to put a blue cord in the tzitzit of the corners. ³⁹ And it shall be to you for a tzitzit, and you shall see it, and shall remember all the commands of YHWH and shall do them, and not search after your own heart and your own eyes after which you went whoring, ⁴⁰ so that you remember, and shall do all my commands, and be set apart unto your Elohim. ⁴¹ I am YHWH your Elohim, who brought you out of the land of Egypt (Mitsrayim), to be your Elohim. I am YHWH your Elohim.*"

A prophecy in the Tanak speaks of the Messiah as follows: "*The Sun of Righteousness shall arise with healing in His wings.*" Malachi 4:2 NKJV. These "wings" are "kanaph" (כָּנָף) in Hebrew, and refer to the edge of a garment, which is the tzitzit. We read in the Gospel according to Luke: "*⁴³ Now a woman, having a flow of blood for twelve years, who had spent all her livelihood on physicians and could not be healed by any, ⁴⁴ came from behind and touched the border of His garment. And immediately her flow of blood stopped.*" Luke 8:43-44 NKJV. The Greek word used to describe a border is "kraspedon" (κρασπεδον) which means a fringe or tassel. In other words, she grabbed His tzitzit that He was wearing in obedience to the Torah. Therefore, He came with healing in His tzitzit just as was foretold by the Prophet Malachi.

Also, in Matthew (Mattithyahu) 14:35-36 we read: "*³⁵ And when the men of that place (Gennesar) recognized Him, they sent out into all that surrounding country, and brought to Him all*

who were sick, ³⁶ *and begged Him to let them only touch the* *tzitzit of His garment. And as many as touched it were* *completely healed.*" We see in these passages not only a beautiful fulfillment of prophecy, but also an example of the Torah observance of Yahushua. This is an aspect of His life has been obscured due to translation inconsistencies and ignorance on the part of Gentile translators.

The Sages teach that there are 613 commandments, also known as mitzvot, found in the Torah. They believe there are 248 positive commandments, which equals the number of important organs in the body. They also believe that there are 365 negative commandments that equals the number of sinews in the body. Therefore, the total number of commandments (613) equals the total number of sinews and organs that make up a man.

This symbolizes the fact that man was created to obey Elohim and perform His will. The numeric equivalent of the word "tzitzit" (ציצית) is 600 (צ = 90; י = 10; צ = 90; י = 10; ת = 400)[34] and the tzitzit are tied with 5 knots and 8 threads on each fringe to make up the other 13. By donning the tallit a person wraps them self in the commandments, which demonstrates his or her obedience and the protective covering which YHWH provides when we live according to His ways.

Therefore, the vision of Kepha has extraordinary significance when viewed in a proper historical, cultural and Scriptural context and in no way supports the common Christian interpretation that YHWH changed His commandments concerning food. The unclean food was symbolic of the Gentile nations that were lowered on a tallit by the four tzitzit. Traditional "Jewish" weddings occur under a "chupah" (חופה), which is a tallit held above

the husband and wife on the four corners. By covering the bride and the bridegroom with the husband's tallit, they are symbolizing that their marriage will be under the protection and authority of YHWH.

There is considerable symbolism concerning the tallit and marriage which stems from an interpretation of Ezekiel (Yehezqel) 16:8: "... *your time was the time of love, and I spread my mantle over you and covered your nakedness. And I swore an oath to you and entered into a covenant with you, and you became Mine . . .*"

In Kepha's vision we can see, the Gentiles being healed or lowered into the fold by the Great Shepard from above by His tzitzit which brings healing to all the nations and we can see the grafting in, or marriage, of the Gentile Converts with the native Yisraelites into the Commonwealth of Yisrael. The Scriptures record that Messiah will return for a Bride who will present herself: "*without stain or wrinkle or any other blemish, but set apart and blameless.*" Ephesians 5:26-28. The passage is stating that the Bride of Messiah, the set apart Assembly, will be clean. The Bride gets clean by the shedding of Messiah's blood and she stays clean by remaining set apart, obedient to the commandments of YHWH which includes the dietary instructions.

6

The Teachings of Messiah

Yahushua never abolished the Torah or the dietary instructions for that matter. He could not have made this fact any clearer when He stated: "*[17] Do not think that I have come to abolish the Torah or the Prophets; I have not come to abolish them but to fulfill them. [18] I tell you the truth, until heaven and earth disappear, not the smallest letter, not the least stroke of a pen, will by any means disappear from the Torah until everything is accomplished. [19] Anyone who breaks one of the least of these commandments and teaches others to do the same will be called least in the kingdom of heaven, but whoever practices and teaches these commands will be called great in the kingdom of heaven. [20] For I tell you that unless your righteousness surpasses that of the Pharisees and the teachers of the law, you will certainly not enter the kingdom of heaven.*" Mattityahu 5:17-20.

Fulfilling the Torah does not mean to abolish, destroy or do away with; rather it means to accomplish or to satisfy. In other words, the Messiah did it perfectly and leads by example. He properly lived and obeyed the Torah and His followers are supposed to follow His pattern and teach others to obey. Since Heaven and earth have not passed away, the Torah is still in effect. If you refuse to obey and teach others not to obey because they are "under grace" then you will be called least in the Kingdom.

It is interesting to study how Yahushua often referred to unclean animals in His parables and ministry to demonstrate the difference between clean and unclean. During one of His teachings He instructed: *"Do not give dogs what is sacred; do not throw your pearls to pigs. If you do, they may trample them under their feet, and then turn and tear you to pieces."* Mattithyahu 7:6 NIV. Both dogs and pigs are unclean animals and we are instructed by Yahushua to distinguish between that which is clean and that which is unclean.

Most people are familiar with the parable of the Prodigal Son found in Luke 15:11-31. The interesting thing to note is that the wayward son left his father's house with  great wealth but soon found himself in a far off country; a stranger living in a strange land, living a sinful life, eventually working for somebody else with unclean animals and eating along side the pigs. Again the Messiah uses pigs to get His point across to emphasize the lifestyle that the lost son was living. In the parable, the son soon realized that his father's servants ate and lived better than himself so he opted to return to his father and live as one of his servants. His father gladly accepted him back with his full stature as a son. He then called for the fatted calf, a clean animal, to be slain and they had a celebration.

As a side note, most people recognize this parable as a teaching on forgiveness, but I believe there may be a deeper meaning to this passage. There were two brothers in this story. The older remained true to his father, continually served him and according to his own testimony, he never transgressed any of the father's commandments at anytime. This is highly  unlikely since he was surely not perfect. So he believed that he was righteous according to his own criteria.

In any event, he got mad because his younger brother sinned and squandered the blessing that his father had given him and now returned to a greater party than had ever been given for the older brother. This parable could very easily apply to the two houses of Yisrael and the reunion which has been prophesied to occur.

While the House of Yahudah, the "Jews", have purportedly kept the Commandments of the Father and diligently served Him, the House of Yisrael was scattered among the nations, and lived with, worked for and ate with the Gentiles (represented by the unclean pigs). They sinned and were expelled from the Land, but one day will realize their mistake and their identity; then they will repent and return to the Father. The Father will clothe the younger son with a fine robe, as Jacob (Yaakob) did with Joseph, and declare a feast, while the older son will resent this treatment because of his supposed service and faithfulness.

Parables typically have meaning beyond the obvious and require revelation to see the deeper message. In the case of the prodigal son, to understand this parable, it is important to understand the restorative work that YHWH has planned for His creation. Every portion of the parable has meaning and the reference to pigs becomes very clear when we realize the symbolism and significance that it has in the light of YHWH's rules of kashrut.

A final example of the use of pigs in the ministry of the Messiah can be found in three of the four Messianic Gospels. Luke provides the following account of the incident:

> "26 They sailed to the region of the Gerasenes, which is across the lake from Galilee. 27 When Yahushua stepped ashore, He was met by a demon-possessed man from the town. For a long time this man had not worn clothes or lived in a house, but had lived in the tombs. 28 When he saw Yahushua, he cried out and fell at his feet, shouting at the top of his voice, 'What do you want with me, Yahushua, Son of the Most High Elohim? I beg you, don't torture me!' 29 For Yahushua had commanded the evil spirit to come out of the man. Many times it had seized him, and though he was chained hand and foot and kept under guard, he had broken his chains and had been driven by the demon into solitary places. 30 Yahushua asked him, 'What is your name?' 'Legion,' he replied, because many demons had gone into him. 31 And they begged him repeatedly not to order them to go into the Abyss. 32 A large herd of pigs was feeding there on the hillside. The demons begged Yahushua to let them go into them, and he gave them permission. 33 When the demons came out of the man, they went into the pigs, and the herd rushed down

the steep bank into the lake and was drowned. [34] When those tending the pigs saw what had happened, they ran off and reported this in the town and countryside, [35] and the people went out to see what had happened. When they came to Yahushua, they found the man from whom the demons had gone out, sitting at Yahushua's feet, dressed and in his right mind; and they were afraid. [36] Those who had seen it told the people how the demon-possessed man had been cured. [37] Then all the people of the region of the Gerasenes asked Yahushua to leave them, because they were overcome with fear. So he got into the boat and left." Luke 8:26-37.

I remember reading that passage and thinking: "I wonder what 'Jesus' had against those poor pigs?" It never

dawned on me that those people never should have been tending those pigs in the first place. They were in the region of the Galilee known as Kursi. They were close to the Decapolis City known as Hippos, and those pigs were probably being raised for people to sacrifice to false gods and eat in direct disobedience to the Torah. We know this from one Gospel passage that states: *"He came through the midst of the region of Decapolis to the Sea of Galilee."* Mark 7:31 NKJV.

"Decapolis was a group of ten cities (as the name implies), most of them on the east side of the Jordan River. The cities of the Decapolis developed a rich Hellenistic culture."[35] It is important to understand that Hellenism involved the adoption of the Greek language and culture which, in large part was pagan. One of the pagan deities worshipped and celebrated in that culture was Dionysus and swine were used for Dionysian sacrifices and meals. The mysteries of Dionysus were practiced in the Decapolis and according to the Book of 2 Maccabees: " . . . *a decree was issued to the neighboring Greek cities (Decapolis), that they should adopt the same policy toward the Jews and make them partake of the (Gentile) sacrifices . . ."* (2 Maccabees 6:8 RSV). Accordingly, there is a powerful implication that the mysteries of Dionysus were still practiced in the Decapolis when Yahushua passed through which presumably prompted his actions. I would imagine that He was tired of His people being led astray by this false religion that encouraged them to commit abominable acts and disregard the Torah.

His act of casting the demons into the pigs was also perfectly consistent with the Torah. He permitted the unclean demons to enter the unclean pigs. He did not allow the demons to enter into clean animals that would be consumed by people observing the dietary instructions. I dare say that if Yahushua intended to do away with the Torah and declare all things clean, then He would not have continued to use pigs in such a consistently negative fashion throughout His teachings and ministry.

It is important to remember that most, if not all, of the people that followed Yahushua and listened to His teachings were Yahudim. By using unclean animals in His parables and ministry He was stressing His point to Torah observant children of Yisrael who understood the

difference between clean and unclean. It is the failure of Christianity to understand this distinction that has created so much doctrinal confusion and so many imbedded contradictions.

7

Food and Modern Society

In this discussion of the dietary instructions I do not mean to focus just on pigs, because there are a lot of things Christians, and Jews, for that matter, eat that are not kosher like shrimp, lobster, clams and the like. Regrettably, swine's flesh has become one of the predominant foods in American society and around the world. I myself am a former swine lover, I can admit that fact. I used to love my bacon in the morning, not too crispy but not too soft either. If no bacon was available, a slab of ham would do nicely. For lunch, a bacon cheeseburger was generally on the menu. Dinner would include a nice filet wrapped with bacon or a rack of baby back ribs, maybe a pulled pork sandwich.

I loved sausage and swine filled cold cuts; you name the pig delicacy and I probably ate it, except the hooves, ears or other parts in jars that you see in the grocery store. I never could figure out exactly who bought those pickled parts, but of course, we all eat them when we consume pork sausage and hot dogs. In fact, the FDA allows hot dogs to contain up to 20 percent animal hair, believe it or not. It was not until I started investigating the dietary

instructions that I discovered this fact. If I had known there was even one animal hair in my hot dogs, I probably would have observed kashrut long ago. Now, thankfully I only eat kosher beef hot dogs, but I still have to watch out for harmful additives that some manufacturers put in their products.

Ever since the eyes of my understanding have been enlightened to this important topic (Ephesians 1:18), I cannot help but wonder what it was about swine that used to be so appetizing. Pigs are one of the filthiest animals alive. Some slaughterhouses have a special section for the cancer ridden pigs that are crippled so badly with tumors they cannot even walk.[36] For goodness sake they will eat anything including their own feces: they will even eat a tumor off of another pig!

Despite this gruesome reality, bits of cooked swine are sprinkled over salads, strips of cooked swine are layered over sandwiches, slabs of cooked swine are eaten for certain Christian Holy Days, their intestines are used for hot dogs and sausage and their flesh and by products are mixed into so many things that, without ingredient labels, it would be difficult to discern whether or not something contains pig. I challenge the reader to start taking note of how many "food" products include pig's flesh, it is simply astonishing how vast this abomination has been perpetrated upon societies, in particular a "Christian" society such as the United States of America.

Swine's flesh is not healthy, no matter how much the pork industry tries to promote it as "the other white meat." "The human body virtually goes into toxic shock by consuming pork. Massive amounts of blood and energy go to the stomach and intestines to help breakdown and digest this toxic material. Pork is never fully digested in the human body; however the human digestive system works nonstop in overdrive for up to eighteen hours attempting to neutralize and digest pork."[37] One of the reasons why pork is so toxic is because "[t]he digestive tract of a pig is completely different from that of a cow. It is similar to a [humans] in that the stomach is very acidic. Pigs are gluttonous, never knowing when to stop eating. Their stomach acids become diluted because of the volume of food, allowing all kinds of vermin to pass through this protective barrier. Parasites, bacteria, viruses and toxins can pass into the pig's flesh because of overeating. These toxins and infectious agents can be passed on to humans when they eat a pig's flesh."[38]

In fact, one particular archaeological study examined the differences between ancient Yisraelite and Egyptian (Mitsrite) toilets. In the Yisraelite households in Yahrushalayim, which presumably observed kosher eating habits, they found no parasites or infectious agents, only pollen from the fruits, vegetables and herbs that they had eaten. On the other hand, Egyptian (Mitsrite) toilets revealed eggs from schistosoma, trichnella, wire worm and tapeworms, all found in pork. All of these organisms cause significant chronic diseases.[39] It is apparent that there are practical health benefits associated with observing kashrut and obedience helps keep us healthy. I know that this message must be especially disturbing to those Believers in the Southern States of America who love their barbeque, but this is a good example of where the appetites and desires of the flesh clash with spiritual things.

Northeasterners are not exempt from their own particular kosher infractions. Being one myself I can testify how much they love their seafood. By the time I was three years old I was shucking my own clams and slurping them down raw by the dozens - steaming them was for sissies. Oysters also tantalized my youthful taste buds. A dash of lemon and a hint of horseradish was all that was needed before I slid the bivalve mollusk down my open throat without even chewing.

My parents never denied me any gastronomic desires of life and allowed me to delve into the world of crustacean culinary delights at an early age. I knew how to get my monies worth at a peel your own shrimp salad bar and I could readily dismember and consume a freshly scalded lobster or crab with lightning speed. My youthful eyes keenly reconnoitered for small pieces of meat hidden in the fragmented shells and my nimble fingers were skilled at dislodging any remaining morsels from their stubborn hold. Rarely did I need the tools of an amateur - the nutcracker and the miniature fork. Why use a fork when you could suck the stray flesh right out of the mutilated corpses arm like a straw!

Little did I know that all of these so-called delicacies are nothing more than deep-sea garbage collectors. They are bottom feeders that sift and eat the refuse and waste that is in the water. "Shellfish can be placed in a body of water that is contaminated with cholera bacteria, and they will purify the  water. Shrimp, oysters, crab, scallops and mussels are particularly efficient at this. They filter large volumes of water every day. Sewage laden with chemicals, toxins and harmful bacteria, parasites and viruses become concentrated in those shellfish. The cause of cholera outbreaks in several areas has been traced to contaminated shrimp, crab, oysters and clams. A recent outbreak of cholera in Central America was related to shellfish ingestion. All this led one researcher to say, 'By far the single greatest danger posed by seafood is from raw shellfish.' The flesh of shellfish is where the disease-causing organisms are found."[40]

Despite gorging on these toxic filled victuals most of my growing years, YHWH mercifully allowed me to avoid serious illness or death and I advance into adulthood 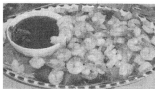 wherein I continued to devour all of my favorite unclean "seafood" cuisine. If you were invited to my home for dinner you would undoubtedly be greeted by an overflowing tray of jumbo shrimp grandly presented on a bed of ice, de-veined of course, lest my guests should have to trouble themselves with extracting the langostino's excrement immediately prior to consuming its hind section.

I would often travel to Maine and eat nothing but lobster at every meal for days on end. The menu would typically include a lobster omelet for breakfast, a lobster roll with a side of lobster chowder for lunch and a fresh whole lobster for dinner or maybe a lazy man's lobster if I didn't want the mess. I think I made my wife ill by the end of our trips and as a result, she stopped eating lobster long before we realized that it was not kosher.

I had a dream one night, not long after I started obeying the dietary instructions, which was similar to that of Shimon Kepha. I saw piles of unclean seafood crawling and oozing in a big slimy heap. I was immediately repulsed by what I saw and I woke up with that continued feeling of nausea. It was like a switch had been turned on and instead of having a fleshly craving for these prohibited items I had

a real revulsion for them.

This was clearly a supernatural culinary conversion that only the Creator of the Cosmos could accomplish with such decisiveness. It was a wonderful example of recognizing how the appetites of our flesh often conflict with the will of the Father and we need Him to help us align our desires with His.

Society has decided to gorge itself on creatures that YHWH has prohibited us from eating. If you want to be obedient to His will then you must be set apart regarding what you eat. After all kashrut is about being like YHWH. We spend a considerable amount of time purchasing, preparing and consuming our meals. It only makes sense that such a pervasive activity would have spiritual lessons and significance.

Another issue that has become increasingly significant is the subject of Genetically Modified Organisms. Also known as GMO's, these organisms involve mankind tampering with the genetic coding of seeds, and even animals. While this is not an issue specifically addressed in kashrut, it should be implicit that we only eat foods designed and created by YHWH.

As a result, we should only eat items containing the original genetic coding of the Creator. Mixing genes and tampering with genes inherently violates the principles contained within the Torah. This is just one of many issues to consider as we examine the ethics of eating.

8

The Ethics of Eating

It is not hard to learn and understand the Scriptural dietary commands. They are not a burden, although as was previously stated, they may clash with the desires of our flesh. Other than the specific types of creatures listed in the Scriptures, an animal may be clean, but if it is not killed in a kosher fashion it is not fit to be food. For instance, a cow is clean but if it is strangled, it is not kosher. Also, a deer is clean, but if it is found dead on the side of the road (road kill) it is not kosher (Vayiqra 7:24, 17:15, 22:8; Debarim 14:21).

You cannot eat a chicken wing if the chicken remains alive. As long as there is life still in the animal you cannot eat of its flesh. This leads to an important part of kashrut involving the treatment of the animal that is being killed and eaten. If nothing else convinces you that kashrut is appropriate for all Believers then the humane treatment of the "food" that you eat should certainly be an important factor.

The simple fact of the matter is that most large industrial slaughterhouses and breeding farms are like torture chambers for animals. From the minute an animal is born it is typically deprived of a normal existence.[41] It is

often fed hormone laced substances, injected with drugs and antibiotics in filthy, overcrowded and unhealthy environments. The animals are generally not treated with any degree of dignity and are often killed using extremely brutal, grotesque and inhumane methods. In fact, it is well-known that when an animal dies in a state of panic, its entire body is flooded with adrenaline, a substance which remains in the tissue after death. Most slaughterhouses create extreme stress in animals before they are killed which is bad for animal and the people that consume, not only the flesh, but the fear of the slaughtered animal. Our Creator does not want us partaking in this process.

For an animal to be kosher under Talmudic tradition, it must not only be one of the species described in the Torah as clean, but it also must be killed in the most humane and painless fashion possible. This tenet is known as "tsaar ba-aley chayyim" and is considered to originate with the Torah. I believe that this ethical commandment in Judaism is consistent with the implicit intention of the Torah.

The ritual slaughter method used in Judaism is known as "shehita" wherein a surgically sharp knife called a "cha'lef" is used by a "Sho'chet" so that the animal barely feels the cut. The esophagus, trachea and neck arteries are severed in one swift and continuous cut that should result in a fast and painless  death so that the animal does not suffer. According to Rabbi Ezra Raful, head of the Israeli Chief Rabbinite's International Shehita Supervision Department: "it normally takes 30 seconds to a minute for [a] cow to lose consciousness if shehita is done properly . . . both of the

major blood vessels are cut at the same time, which cuts off all blood to the brain immediately, and the cow feels nothing."[42]

This does not mean that all kosher slaughterhouses are immune from scrutiny and criticism. There have been documented instances of kosher slaughter houses that have not treated animals in a humane fashion.[43] The important thing is that kashrut is supposed to support and promote the humane treatment of animals which often stands in stark contrast to the methods used in the modern commercial meat industry.

If a slaughterhouse is kosher then the chances are good that the methods used are humane and the animals are treated better than in commercial slaughterhouses where, although things are currently not as bad as the industry described in *The Jungle* by Upson Sinclair, they still fall far short from the standards demanded by kashrut.

At present, there are a number of different watchdog groups with varying political agendas and tactics that I may not necessarily agree with. Regardless, they may offer useful information concerning the treatment of animals throughout the world.

I believe that generally, every person has their own set of dietary regulations. Therefore everyone observes kashrut to some extent. In other words, everybody has their own list of things that they have determined to be edible, and they have a list of things that they consider detestable. The only question is whether their list lines up with YHWH's list. For instance, I would bet that most people would object to drinking a glass of blood or eating a bat, which is consistent with the Torah.

Many people may, in fact, follow the Scriptural dietary instructions without even realizing it. Vegans will

likely not run afoul of the commandments, although that may not be their goal. This really only becomes an issue when the appetites and desires of an individual's pallet clash with the ordinances of YHWH. At that point, a decision must be made whether to choose one's own ways or the ways of YHWH.

There is no doubt that we live in a society obsessed with eating, health and diet. What I find amazing is that the Creator of the universe and all mankind has expressly instructed us how to eat and those instructions go largely ignored, except for some Torah observant "Jews" and Messianic Believers. No wonder there is so much disease and sickness in society. It goes without question that it is the failure to follow the Torah that has resulted in the proliferation of many diseases we now see throughout the world. There are countless illnesses and sexually transmitted diseases that are spread by violating the Torah instructions regarding sexual conduct, diet and cleanliness.

Society is now passing off as "food" that which is considered abominable by YHWH. There is no question that most chronic diseases in society are the result of poor diet and I believe that failure to follow kashrut dietary habits is the source of many of the health problems in the

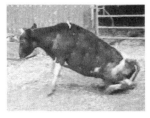 world. The sudden concern over bovine spongiform encephalopathy (BSE), also known as mad cow disease, is a good example. A cow is clean because it has a split hoof and "chews the cud".[44] If they eat properly and are killed in the proper manner, they are then fit for food. Regrettably, man has decided to feed ground up animals to beef cattle that is resulting in the spread of deadly diseases.

Scientists have now found that farm raised salmon are being fed unclean fish and other pollutants which are not a part of their regular diet in the wild. As a result, people are more likely to consume a cancer causing poison from a salmon raised by men than from one caught in its natural habitat. In fact, the average dioxin level in farmed-raised salmon was 11 times higher than that in wild salmon.[45] This and BSE are just two small examples of the tampering which is done to "food" resulting in health problems of epidemic proportions.

It is well known that "swine are good incubators of toxic parasites and viruses. A scientist at the University of Giessen's Institute of Virology in Germany showed in a study of worldwide influenza epidemics that pigs are the one animal that can serve as a mixing vessel for new influenza viruses that may seriously threaten world health. If a pig is exposed to a human's DNA virus and then a bird's virus, the pig mixes the two viruses – developing a new DNA virus that is often extremely lethal for humans. These viruses have already caused worldwide epidemics and destruction. Virologists have concluded that if we do not find a way to separate humans from pigs, the whole earth's population may be at risk."[46]

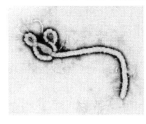

We are currently witnessing outbreaks of new diseases and viruses such as Ebola, SARS (Severe Acute Respiratory Syndrome), the Influenza A (H5N1) and H7N9 avian influenza, among others. The 2014 Ebola outbreak in western Africa was directly linked to the consumption of "bush meat" consisting of animals such as monkeys and bats.

Some suggest pigs could be involved in transmitting other viruses from chickens to humans. I find it interesting that one journalist from NPR (National Public Radio) actually admitted that the reason why SARS was contained in 2003 was because the Scriptural method of quarantining infected individuals was implemented.[47] Sadly, this appears to be more by coincidence than design because there does not seem to be any reversion to Scriptural principles in any other form.

As a result, the world will likely experience new and expanded health crisis in the years to come. As mankind continues to thwart the commandments of YHWH and tamper with His perfect order, things will continue to get worse. Herbicides, pesticides, hormones, antibiotics, additives, coloring, preservatives and various forms of food processing are all resulting in the poisoning of the populace. They are wreaking havoc of the immune systems of mankind making them ever more vulnerable to sickness and disease.

Instead of correcting our diets to resolve these problems the government and corporations would rather spend trillions of dollars on new drugs, vaccines and chemicals to deal with the symptoms of this mass poisoning. Sadly, these drugs do not heal people, they only make a persons unhealthy condition more tolerable.

As a culture, we have developed a medicine mentality; when we get sick we run to the medicine cabinet, the doctor or the nearest urgent care clinic. By doing so we are in danger of committing the sin of Asa by seeking a prescription or a physician for healing, rather than seeking YHWH. (2 Chronicles 16:12).

9

Blessings and Curses

YHWH promised Yisrael that if they obeyed Him, they would not get any of the disease of the Egyptians (Mitsrites). *"If you diligently heed the voice of YHWH your Elohim and do what is right in His sight, give ear to His commandments and keep all His statutes, I will put none of the diseases on you which I have brought on the Egyptians (Mitsrites). For I am YHWH who heals you."* Shemoth 15:26. In fact, the Scriptures record that previously, when the children of Yisrael left Egypt (Mitsrayim) not one of them were sick. (Tehillim 105:37). I believe that they were healed by their obedience in partaking of the Passover meal.

Christianity is filled with sick and diseased Believers who may be suffering simply as a result of their disobedience. The answer to their problem may be in the very "Bible" which they carry with them to service every Sunday; that same "Bible" which is rarely opened to the pages containing the dietary commands. The Prophet Hoshea hit the nail on the head when he proclaimed: *"My people are destroyed from lack of knowledge. Because you have rejected knowledge, I also reject you as my priests; because you have ignored the Torah of Elohim, I also will ignore your children."* Hoshea 4:6.

If you consider yourself to be a Believer and follower of the Messiah of Yisrael, then you are a priest and you are supposed to act like a priest by obeying the Torah, not ignoring the Torah as most of Christianity has done through the centuries.

Read what Shaul has to say about how we should treat our bodies: "*¹⁹ Do you not know that your body is the temple of the Holy Spirit who is in you, whom you have from Elohim, and you are not your own? ²⁰ For you were bought at a price; therefore glorify Elohim in your body and in your spirit, which are Elohim's.*" 1 Corinthians 6:19-20. Shaul again reiterates this concept in his second letter to the Corinthians: "*¹⁶ What agreement is there between the temple of Elohim and idols? For we are the temple of the living Elohim. As Elohim has said: 'I will live with them and walk among them, and I will be their Elohim, and they will be My people. ¹⁷ Therefore come out from them and be separate', says YHWH. 'Touch no unclean thing, and I will receive you. ¹⁸ I will be a Father to you, and you will be my sons and daughters', says YHWH El Shaddai.*" 2 Corinthians 6:16-18.

If you believe in YHWH Elohim then you have the future hope of receiving a new body, but for the time being you still reside on this planet in your body of flesh. That body is a temple or "dwelling place" and must be kept clean, both inside and out. Just as it was considered an abomination to slaughter a pig on the Brazen Altar in the Temple of YHWH as was done by the Seleucid ruler Antiochus Epiphanes IV in 168 B.C.E., so too it is abominable to put an unclean animal in the body of a Spirit Filled Believer, which is the Temple of Elohim.

If I might be so bold, I would encourage the reader to start being obedient in regard to YHWH's dietary instructions before going to the next healing service to seek a cure for your illness. That very act of obedience may be what is needed to break the bondage of sickness on your body. While we are saved by faith, **we are blessed by obedience.**

Good health testifies to sound doctrine in your life. If you want to live a blessed and healthy life according to the promises found within the Torah, you need to be obedient. Your failure to obey the Torah may be the reason that your prayers have not been answered because: *"one who turns away his ear from hearing the Torah, even his prayer is an abomination."* Proverbs (Mishle) 28:9. If you are ignoring the Torah and participating in abominable acts, even your prayers are an abomination to YHWH.

The Scriptures are very clear that disobedience results in sickness and disease. *"[58] If you do not carefully observe all the words of this Torah that are written in this book, that you may fear this glorious and awesome Name, YHWH your Elohim, [59] then YHWH will bring upon you and your descendants extraordinary plagues - **great and prolonged plagues - and serious and prolonged sicknesses.**[60] Moreover He will bring back on you all the diseases of Mitsrayim, of which you were afraid, **and they shall cling to you.**[61] **Also every sickness and every plague, which is not written in the book of this Torah, will YHWH bring upon you until you are destroyed."** Debarim 28:58-61.*

This word is just as relevant today as it was when it was spoken thousands of years ago. If you are a partaker in the Covenant of YHWH and belong in His Kingdom, then you are subject to the Torah. Those sickness, plagues and diseases are just as applicable to the rebellious Assembly of Believers of this age as they were to the ancient Assembly

of Yisrael

The Messianic Scriptures confirm that there are clearly illnesses that are the result of transgressing the Torah. The Great Physician Yahushua who is able to heal every sickness and disease (Mattithyahu 9:35) revealed this when He said to the sick man: "*See, you have been made well. Sin no more, lest a worse thing come upon you.*" John 5:4 NKJV. The word sin means to transgress the commandments of YHWH. Therefore, Yahushua was indicating that the man's illness was the result of his transgressions and in order to stay healthy he needed to obey. This is in direct contradiction to popular Christian doctrine that teaches the Messiah abolished the Torah through grace.

Of course, there are things that require a supernatural touch from YHWH, but we often bring on a lot of the problems in our lives simply because of our disobedience. If you have considered the issue of kashrut and its application to your life and you decide not to follow the dietary instructions, then you are putting your own desires above YHWH's.

With that type of attitude you should not expect your prayers to be answered nor should you expect to receive the blessings of YHWH. "*Your iniquities have turned these things away, and your sins have withheld good from you.*" Jeremiah (Yirmeyahu) 5:25. Your willful disobedience will simply result in your prayers not being answered, and you will not receive the good things that YHWH has for you. As with most things, YHWH Elohim is patient with us while we remain ignorant, but when He reveals His truth, it is important that we respond with obedience.

10

Passover and the Feast of Unleavened Bread

In the last Chapter the subject of the Passover (Pesach) was discussed in the context of healing the Yisraelites who partook in the meal. The Passover is an Appointed Time called a "moadi" (מועדי) in Hebrew. The account of the Passover is provided as follows:

"¹ YHWH said to Mosheh and Aharon in Mitsrayim, ² This new moon is to be for you the first new moon, the first new moon of your year. ³ Tell the whole community of Yisrael that on the tenth day of this month each man is to take a lamb for his family, one for each household. ⁴ If any household is too small for a whole lamb, they must share one with their nearest neighbor, having taken into account the number of people there are. You are to determine the amount of lamb needed in accordance with what each person will eat. ⁵ The animals you choose must be year-old males without defect, and you may take them from the sheep or the goats. ⁶ Take care of them until the fourteenth day of the month, when all the people of the community of Yisrael must slaughter them between the evenings. ⁷ Then they

are to take some of the blood and put it on the sides and tops of the doorframes of the houses where they eat the lambs. ⁸ That same night they are to eat the meat roasted over the fire, along with bitter herbs, and bread made without yeast. ⁹ Do not eat the meat raw or cooked in water, but roast it over the fire -head, legs and inner parts. ¹⁰ Do not leave any of it till morning; if some is left till morning, you must burn it. ¹¹ This is how you are to eat it: with your cloak tucked into your belt, your sandals on your feet and your staff in your hand. Eat it in haste; it is YHWH's Passover. ¹² On that same night I will pass through Mitsrayim and strike down every firstborn - both men and animals - and I will bring judgment on all the gods of Mitsrayim. I am YHWH. ¹³ The blood will be a sign for you on the houses where you are; and when I see the blood, I will pass over you. No destructive plague will touch you when I strike Mitsrayim. ¹⁴ **This is a day you are to commemorate; for the generations to come you shall celebrate it as a festival to YHWH - a lasting ordinance.** ¹⁵ For seven days you are to eat bread made without yeast. **On the first day remove the yeast from your houses, for whoever eats anything with yeast in it from the first day through the seventh must be cut off from Yisrael.** ¹⁶ On the first day hold a set apart assembly, and another one on the seventh day. Do no work at all on these days, except to prepare food for everyone to eat--that is all you may do." Shemot 12:1-16

Notice that the Passover is a perpetual commandment, it is to be kept forever and not just by those practicing Judaism, but by all who rely on the shed blood of the "Passover Lamb" for their redemption. The Apostle Shaul even gave instructions on the spiritual parallels provided by the feast. *"[6] Don't you know that a little leaven leavens the entire lump? [7] Therefore cleanse out the old leaven, so that you are a new lump, as you are unleavened. For Messiah, our Passover Lamb, has been slaughtered. [8] Therefore let us keep the Festival, not with the old leaven, the leaven of malice and wickedness, but with bread without leaven (matzah), the bread of sincerity and truth."* 1 Corinthians 5:6-8.

As you can see, the Passover is intimately connected with the Feast of Unleavened Bread (Hag Matzah) and both involve particular dietary instructions. During the Passover meal we are commanded to eat roasted lamb and bitter herbs and throughout these times we are commanded not to eat leaven, commonly known as yeast.

Anyone who eats leaven during the Feast is subject

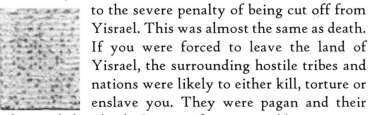

to the severe penalty of being cut off from Yisrael. This was almost the same as death. If you were forced to leave the land of Yisrael, the surrounding hostile tribes and nations were likely to either kill, torture or enslave you. They were pagan and their religions led to death. So even if you were able to survive, your pagan lifestyle would eventually end up in death.

The penalty is repeated again later in the same passage: *"[19] ... whoever eats anything with yeast in it must be cut off from the community of Yisrael, whether he is an alien or native-born. [20] Eat nothing made with yeast. Wherever you live, you must eat unleavened bread."* Shemot 12:19-20. Again, we see that the Torah was equally applicable to the native born Yisraelite and the alien who dwelled with them.

Also, failure of an eligible person to partake of the Passover meal was subject to the same penalty of being cut off. *"But if a man who is ceremonially clean and not on a journey fails to celebrate the Passover, that person must be cut off from his people because he did not present YHWH's offering at the appointed time. That man*

will bear the consequences of his sin." Bemidbar 9:13. If you are a part of the Commonwealth of Yisrael, the only excuse for not eating the Passover at the appointed time is if you are unclean.

This leads to another aspect of kosher that was discussed previously. You cannot partake of the Passover if you are unclean so it is critical that you understand the distinction between clean and unclean. The Children of Yisrael understood this distinction and YHWH made provision as follows: *"⁴ So Mosheh told the Yisraelites to celebrate the Passover, ⁵ and they did so in the Desert of Sinai at twilight on the fourteenth day of the first month. The Yisraelites did everything just as YHWH commanded Mosheh. ⁶ But some of them could not celebrate the Passover on that day because they were unclean on account of a dead body. So they came to Mosheh and Aharon that same day ⁷ and said to Mosheh, 'We have become unclean because of a dead body, but why should we be kept from presenting YHWH's offering with the other Yisraelites at the appointed time?' ⁸ Mosheh answered them, 'Wait until I find out what YHWH commands concerning you.'*

⁹ Then YHWH said to Mosheh, ¹⁰ 'Tell the Yisraelites: When any of you or your descendants are unclean because of a being or are away on a journey, they may still celebrate YHWH's Passover. ¹¹ They are to celebrate it on the fourteenth day of the second month between the evenings. They are to eat the lamb, together with unleavened bread and bitter herbs.'" Bemidbar 9:4-11.

You must be clean to partake in the Passover meal. If you are not clean in the first month, then YHWH made provision for the second month. This is exactly what happened during the restoration under King Hezekiah. *"¹⁶ The priests went into the sanctuary of YHWH to purify it. They brought out to the courtyard of YHWH's House everything unclean that they found in the House of YHWH. The Levites*

took it and carried it out to the Kidron Valley. ¹⁷ They began the consecration on the first day of the first month, and by the eighth day of the month they reached the portico of YHWH. For eight more days they consecrated the House of YHWH itself, finishing on the sixteenth day of the first month." 2 Chronicles 29:16-17.

They did not cleanse the Temple in time to celebrate the Passover at the appointed time. *"² The king and his officials and the whole assembly in Yahrushalayim decided to celebrate the Passover in the second month. ³ They had not been able to celebrate it at the regular time because not enough priests had consecrated themselves and the people had not assembled in Yahrushalayim. ⁴ The plan seemed right both to the king and to the whole assembly. ⁵ They decided to send a proclamation throughout Yisrael, from Beersheba to Dan, calling the people to come to Yahrushalayim and celebrate the Passover to YHWH, the Elohim of Yisrael. It had not been celebrated in large numbers*

according to what was written." 2 Chronicles 30:2-5.

The Scriptures report that a very large crowd of people assembled to celebrate, even those from the Northern Tribes. It is important to remember that this was during a time when Yisrael was divided. The Northern Tribes - The House of Yisrael had separated from the Southern Tribes - The House of Yahudah. Many of those from the Northern Tribes were not clean, but they were zealous to partake of the Passover.

"[17] Since many in the crowd had not consecrated themselves, the Levites had to kill the Passover lambs for all those who were not ceremonially clean and could not consecrate their lambs to YHWH. [18] Although most of the many people who came from Ephraim, Manasseh, Issachar and Zebulun had not purified themselves, yet they ate the Passover, contrary to what was written. But Hezekiah prayed for them, saying, 'May YHWH, who is good, pardon everyone [19] who sets his heart on seeking Elohim - YHWH, the Elohim of his fathers - even if he is not clean according to the cleansing of the set apart place.' [20] **And YHWH heard Hezekiah and healed the people.***"* 2 Chronicles 30:17-20.

Notice YHWH healed the people who would have otherwise been cursed for their disobedience. This is just another example of how our eating habits have spiritual and physical consequences.

II

In the End

In general, clean animals eat those things that both man and beast were intended to eat from the beginning of time. Unclean animals tend to be predators, scavengers or bottom feeders. They all typically eat vile and detestable things that are not kosher or fit for humans to eat, and they typically contain much higher levels of toxicity than those creatures which are considered clean.[52] YHWH created them to keep the planet clean and then warned us not to eat them. These instructions are for our own good and YHWH is really not being unreasonable by denying us of these unhealthy items - He is actually trying to protect us.

I liken the dietary instructions to a parent limiting a child's intake of processed foods and sweets. If you let your child eat nothing but junk food when you know it is bad for their health you would not be considered a very good parent.

Children do not usually understand why their parents deprive them of their favorite sugar filled treats and genetically modified snack foods, but nevertheless, it is for their own good and if they are obedient, they will have healthy teeth and healthy bodies that will serve them well throughout their lives.

I want my children to eat well and enjoy their meals as does our Creator. In fact, to eat and drink and find satisfaction in all our toil is a gift from Elohim. (Ecclesiastes 3:13).

As a Heavenly Father giving advice to His children, the Creator of the universe gives us guidance concerning what we put into our bodies. This guidance is meant for our own good and our obedience allows Him to bless us. Hear the words of the Father as He counsels His child: *"¹ My son, do not forget my Torah, but let your heart keep My commands; ² For length of days and long life and peace they will add to you."* Mishle 3:1-2.

It should now be obvious that kashrut is meant to bless and not to restrict us. It is guidance from a loving Father who wants the best for His children. All that it takes is ears to hear and a heart to obey in order to receive those blessings.

I hope by now that it is clear to the reader that kashrut is important, but it is much more than a health issue. The Scriptures repeatedly liken food to sound doctrine (John 4:32, Hebrews 5:12-14) and the Messiah said that His food was *"to do the will of Him who sent me and to finish his work."* John 4:34. He directly relates food with His Will and His Word. He even calls Himself "the Bread of Life." John 6:48. There is no reason to believe that any of these teachings changed after His resurrection.

In fact, He was raised from the dead to cleanse us and prepare us as containers so that the Spirit of YHWH could dwell within us. As vessels and those who carry the vessels of YHWH we are not to touch any unclean thing. (Isaiah (Yeshayahu) 52:11). It is absurd to think that the death of the Messiah in any way changed YHWH's standard for clean and unclean and an important aspect of

the life of any Believer should be to nurture their awareness between clean and unclean, not only in spiritual matters, but physical as well. We are encouraged to preserve our "*spirit, soul and body*" and remain blameless until the return of Messiah. (1 Thessalonians 1:23). Part of preserving our bodies is observing kashrut and keeping them clean by refraining from ingesting anything abominable.

To emphasize how important it is to obey the dietary instructions let us take a look at some Scriptures that show how YHWH feels about those who do not obey His commandments regarding food. "*1 I revealed Myself to those who did not ask for Me; I was found by those who did not seek Me. To a nation that did not call on My Name, I said, 'Here am I, here am I.' 2 All day long I have held out My hands to an obstinate people, who walk in ways not good, pursuing their own imaginations - 3 a people who continually provoke me to my very face, offering sacrifices in gardens and burning incense on altars of brick; 4 who sit among the graves and spend their nights keeping secret vigil; who eat the flesh of pigs, and whose pots hold broth of unclean meat; 5 who say, 'Keep away; don't come near me, for I am too sacred for you!' Such people are smoke in My nostrils, a fire that keeps burning all day.*" Isaiah (Yeshayahu) 65:1-5.

This Scripture directly refers to Yisrael, but it also can apply to those who ascribe to traditional Christian doctrine. Mainstream Christians are a people that may talk about the Name of YHWH, but they do not call on the Name of YHWH. They are obstinate. They walk in their own ways, contrary to the commandments of YHWH and pursue their own method of sacrifice, worship and conducting "Church"[48] which is not in accordance with His commandments. They ignore His Appointed Times and celebrate their own pagan feasts.[49] They continually

provoke YHWH by claiming to serve Him yet they reject His Torah and the commandments of Torah. They profane His Sabbath, they replace His Name with a title, they replace the Name of His Son with an incorrect Hellenized Greek name,[50] they fail to obey the dietary instructions and they often demonstrate spiritual elitism. They are smoke in the nostrils of YHWH and the fact that this passage specifically speaks of violating the commandments concerning food demonstrates that kashrut is important to YHWH, not just some trivial legalistic matter.

It is crucial that Believers get their lives in order before it is too late. The final chapter of Yeshayahu shows how YHWH perceives mankind in the last days. He actually categorizes people by whether or not they keep kashrut. "*[15] See, YHWH is coming with fire, and his chariots are like a whirlwind; He will bring down his anger with fury, and his rebuke with flames of fire. [16] For with fire and with his sword YHWH will execute judgment upon all men, and many will be those slain by YHWH. [17] Those who consecrate and purify themselves to go into the gardens, following the one in the midst of those who eat the flesh of pigs and rats and other abominable things - they will meet their end together, declares YHWH.*" Yeshayahu 66:15-17.

There is a great banquet feast coming and abominable food will not be on the menu, nor will those who eat abominable things be invited to dine with the King.[51] The unclean will be outside the gates. (Revelation 22:15). Therefore, if you want to sit and eat in the Kingdom, I suggest that you get used to the *carte du jour*.

Faced with all of these Scripture references, the following question must be posed to the Believer that does not obey the Torah or keep kashrut: Did YHWH call something abominable and unclean in the Tanak and then call it clean in the Messianic Scriptures? Did the death and resurrection of the Messiah change the distinction between clean and unclean? The answer to both of these questions is a resounding – NO. Those things that were declared unclean are still unclean. (Revelation 18:2).

Why would the death and resurrection of Messiah make something that was abominable now suddenly acceptable? The answer is that it did not. What YHWH declared abominable is still abominable. In fact, in the Revelation according to John, the Messiah actually chastised the Assemblies of Pergamum and Thyatira for their false doctrines related to their eating. (Revelation 2:14, 2:20). He never abrogated the dietary laws, and He still expects His followers to abide by the commandments.

To make this point clear it may be helpful to look at some of the things declared to be abominable in the Tanak. Vayiqra Chapter 11 uses the word abomination 10 times to describe unclean creatures that are not to be eaten. The word abomination is also used throughout the Scriptures to describe conduct which is not acceptable to YHWH.

The Scriptures declare homosexuality to be an abomination. (Vayiqra 20:13) and provides a penalty of death for such conduct. Idolatry is described as an abomination. (Debarim 7:25-26) and the penalty is death. (Debarim 17:2-6). Witchcraft and sorcery are both considered to be an abomination (Debarim 18:9-14) and both are subject to the penalty of death. (Vayiqra 20:27).

The Proverbs (Mishle) provide a list of things that are considered an abomination. "*16 These six things YHWH hates, yes, seven are an abomination to Him: 17 A proud look, a lying tongue, hands that shed innocent blood, 18 A heart that devises wicked plans, feet that are swift in running to evil, 19 a false witness who speaks lies, and one who sows discord among*

brethren." Mishle 6:16-19. There is no place for any of this conduct in the Kingdom of YHWH.

The foregoing list is by no means exhaustive. I would invite the reader to conduct their own survey of the Scriptures to examine those things that YHWH calls an abomination, although I hope that the point is resoundingly clear. These things are *still* abominable in the eyes of YHWH. The shed blood of the Messiah can provide atonement for these abominations, but they are nonetheless *still* abominations. Therefore, if homosexuality, idolatry, witchcraft, sorcery, pride, lying and the like are *still* abominations, then so is the ingestion of abominable things.

Now let us look at what the Messianic Scriptures have to say about the abominable. "*But the cowardly, unbelieving, **abominable**, murderers, sexually immoral, sorcerers, idolaters, and all liars shall have their part in the lake which burns with fire and brimstone, which is the second death.*" Revelation 21:8 NKJV. "*For we have spent enough of our past lifetime in doing the will of the Gentiles - when we walked in lewdness, lusts, drunkenness, revelries, drinking parties, and abominable idolatries.*" 1 Kepha 4:3-4 NKJV. It is apparent from the Messianic Scriptures that a Believer in Yahushua should not be doing abominable things.

Every Christian should take heed of the following warning. "*¹⁵ To the pure all things are pure, but to those who are defiled and unbelieving nothing is pure; but even their mind and conscience are defiled.¹⁶ **They profess to know Elohim, but in works they deny Him, being abominable, disobedient, and disqualified for every good work.**" Titus 1:15-16.

Your works are your conduct and they reveal your treatment of the Torah. There are many Christians who

profess to know "Elohim" but their actions betray them. YHWH, the Elohim of Yisrael demands obedience and right living as prescribed in the Torah. The false "god" of this world says that you can do whatever feels right or whatever you "feel led" to do, or even eat whatever you want to because you are "under grace." These are all lies contrary to the truth in the Scriptures.

It is necessary for every individual to examine their life and determine the god that they serve. Are you pursuing the lusts of your flesh by eating whatever you desire? Are you gladly accepting the false doctrine that "the Law" is abolished because you do not want to obey the Torah of YHWH or have you simply been ignorant as I was most of my life?

These distinctions are found within the Torah and deal not only with food, but also sexual conduct and most importantly, the heart. (Tehillim 51:10). These issues of the heart go beyond what you eat. They ultimately help to reveal whether or not you have a desire to obey.

This is the heart that YHWH is seeking in a people that He can call His own. He is gathering together a royal priesthood, a people who understand and respect the difference between clean and unclean – a people who are set apart and Kosher.

Endnotes

[1] The words "Jewish", "Jews" and "Jew" are in italics because they are ambiguous and sometimes derogatory terms. At times these expressions are used to describe all of the genetic descendants of Yaakob while at other times the words describe adherents to the religion called Judaism. The terms are commonly applied to ancient Yisraelites as well as modern day descendents of those tribes, whether they are atheists or Believers in YHWH. The word "Jew" originally referred to a member of the tribe of Judah (Yahudah) or a person that lived in the region of Judea. After the different exiles of the House of Yisrael and the House of Yahudah, it was the Yahudim that returned to the land while the House of Yisrael was scattered to the ends of the earth (Yirmeyahu 9:16). Since the House of Yahudah represented the recognizable descendents of Yaakob and, with the House of Yisrael in exile, over time the Yahudim came to represent Yisrael and thus the word "Jew" was used as a general term to describe a Yisraelite. While this label became common and customary, it is not accurate and is the cause of tremendous confusion. This subject is described in greater detail in the Walk in the Light Series book entitled "The Redeemed".

[2] YHWH is the English spelling of the Hebrew tetragrammaton (יהוה) which is the Name of the Creator of the Universe. A detailed discussion of the Name is found in the Walk in the Light Series book entitled "Names".

[3] Rabbinic Judaism has continued a tradition developed by ancient sects of Yisraelites which involves building "a fence around the Torah" (ie. the first five books of Mosheh). The goal is to create rules, regulations and Scriptural interpretations which go beyond the instructions and commandments found within the Torah so as to keep adherents far away from breaking an actual commandment.

[4] Whether or not a food bears the seal of kashrut is not, in and of itself, indicative of the fact that the food meets the criterion set forth in the Scriptures. There are numerous man-made rules and regulations which the Rabbis consider in making

their judgment and interpretation and ultimately, it is the Scriptures which are controlling. However, in this day of modern food processing it can be very useful to have the assurance of a Rabbi that an item of food is kosher and I rely on this system for much of my families food purchasing and consumption.

5   The Mishnah (מסנה) is "the first, and basic, part of the Talmud and the written basis of religious authority for traditional Judaism. The Mishnah contains a written collection of traditional laws (halakoth) handed down orally from teacher to student. It was compiled across a period of about 335 years, from 200 BCE to 135 CE. The Mishnah is grouped into 63 treatises, or tractates, that deal with all areas of Jewish life-legal, theological, social, and religious-as taught in the schools of Palestine. Soon after the Mishnah was compiled, it became known as the "iron pillar of the Torah," since it preserves the way a Jew can follow the Torah. For many Jews, the Mishnah ranks second only to the canon of the Hebrew Scriptures. Indeed, many Jews consider it part of the Torah. Because it is the core for both the Jerusalem Talmud and the Babylonian Talmud, the Mishnah serves as a link between Jews in the land of Israel and Jews scattered around the world." (Nelson's Illustrated Bible Dictionary, Copyright (c) 1986, Thomas Nelson Publishers).

6   The Talmud (תלמוד) is "a collection of books and commentary compiled by Jewish rabbis from A.D. 250 AD - 500 AD. The Hebrew word "Talmud" means "study" or "learning." This is a fitting title for a work that is a library of Jewish wisdom, philosophy, history, legend, astronomy, dietary laws, scientific debates, medicine, and mathematics. The Talmud is made up of interpretation and commentary of the Mosaic and rabbinic law contained in the Mishnah." (Nelson's Illustrated Bible Dictionary, Copyright (c) 1986, Thomas Nelson Publishers).

7   Midrash (מדרס) has been defined as "any of a group of Jewish commentaries on the Hebrew Scriptures written between A.D. 400 AD and A.D. 1200 AD. The word Midrash is based on a Hebrew word that means "to search out." The implication is that of discovering a thought or truth not seen

on the surface-therefore a study, commentary, or homiletical exposition. These commentaries are a collection of public sermons, stories, legal discussions, and meditations on the books of the Bible used during the festivals for public worship in the synagogues. Midrashim (plural of Midrash) were written in Israel and Babylon by the rabbis. Some Midrashim are contained in the Babylonian Talmud; others are part of independent collections of commentaries. There are two types of Midrash: Halakah ("law" or "tradition"), an interpretation of the laws of the Scriptures, and Haggadah ("narration"), the non-legal, or homiletical, part of the Talmud." (Nelson's Illustrated Bible Dictionary, Copyright (c) 1986, Thomas Nelson Publishers)

[8] Yisrael is the English transliteration for the Hebrew word ישראל often spelled Israel.

[9] Elohim is the proper Hebrew word that is often translated "God" and refers to the Creator of the Universe described in the Hebrew and Christian Scriptures. Elohim is plural unlike God, which is singular.

[10] Hawah is the proper transliteration for the Hebrew name (הוה), the wife of Adam, commonly called Eve.

[11] *Vita Adae Et Evae* i 1 - xxii 2 from the Apocrypha and Pseudepigrapha of the Old Testament, R.H. Charles, Oxford: Clarendon Press, 1913 (names and titles corrected by author for consistency).

[12] Canonization is a man-made concept that determines whether certain writings are included within the accepted Scriptures. The canonization of the modern day Bible took place at the Council of Laodicea in Phrygia Pacatiana somewhere between 343 CE and 381 CE. A commonly accepted date is 364 CE, although no one can say for certain when the Synod took place. This subject is addressed in detail in the Walk in the Light Series book entitled "Scriptures."

[13] The Torah (תורה) contains the first five books of the Hebrew and Christian Scriptures. It was written by Moses (Mosheh) and is often referred to as "The Law" in many modern English translations. Law is a very harsh, cold word that often results in the Torah being confused with the Laws, customs and traditions of the religious leaders as well as the laws of

particular countries. The Torah is more accurately defined as the "instruction" of YHWH for His set apart people. The Torah contains instruction for those who desire to live righteous, set apart lives in accordance with the will of YHWH. Contrary to popular belief, people can obey the Torah. (Debarim 30:11-14). It is the myriads of regulations, customs and traditions that men attach to the Torah that make it impossible for people to obey. Also, we do not obey the Torah in order to attain salvation for "all have sinned and fall short of the esteem of Elohim" and we are saved by grace. Rather we follow the Torah because of our desire to be obedient and set apart children of the Living Elohim.

[14] *Panorama of Creation*, Carl E. Baugh, Ph.D., Creation Evidences Museum 1989.

[15] *The Chumash*, The Stone Edition, Rabbi Nosson Scherman, Mesorah Publications, Ltd. 2000 p. 41.

[16] The Tanak is the compilation of Scriptures commonly referred to as The Hebrew Bible or The Old Testament in Christian Bibles. It consists of the Torah (Law), Nebi'im (Prophets) and the Kethubim (Writings), thus the Hebrew acronym TNK, which is pronounced tah-nach.

[17] Grafted in is an expression used by Paul (Shaul) in Chapter 11 of the Letter to the Romans. He continues the metaphor that is made in prophesy, which identifies the House of Yisrael and the House of Yahudah with an Olive Tree. (Yirmeyahu 11:16). Thus Shaul is clearly teaching that we all must become part of this Olive Tree, which is the Yisrael of Elohim, not a church, or new religion. This is where Christianity goes awry, when it teaches that it is a new religion that has replaced Yisrael. You cannot replace Yisrael, you can only join Yisrael and by Yisrael I do not mean the Modern State of Israel which was formed by a resolution of the United Nations. I mean Yisrael, the Elect of YHWH which He created from the beginning of time and which the Messiah will return to take as a Bride.

[18] The term "Messianic Scriptures" is used to describe the Scriptures commonly referred to as the "New Testament". This is done in order to avoid the "old" versus "new" categorization that often juxtaposes the Scriptures against one

another and tends to diminish the power and significance of the Tanak. Contrary to popular belief in Christian circles, the "New Testament" Scriptures did not change the "Old Testament" Scriptures. Yahushua refreshed the first covenant and renewed it by shedding His own blood. He did not abolish the Tanak, instead He filled it full of meaning. (Mattityahu 5:17).

[19] The Jerusalem Council is the common label for the meeting of early Believers held in Yahrushalayim to discuss a controversy that had arisen within the Assembly involving circumcision. The issue was not necessarily whether converts should be circumcised after becoming "saved", but whether circumcision was a necessary step toward salvation. The people who were advocating this position were probably sincere in their belief because circumcision had traditionally always been a fundamental step in the conversion process when a person became a Yisraelite. The bottom line on this subject is that there is no act, outside of faith, which a man can do to bring about his own salvation. Salvation is a free gift so that no one can boast. (Ephesians 2:9; Galatians 6:13). And even our faith comes from Elohim, so quite simply, we cannot boast at all concerning our position. All we can do is give thanks and endeavor to walk in His footsteps.

[20] This dictate is again repeated in Acts 21:25 but most English Translations do a very poor job translating the Greek text. Some actually add numerous words that are not in the Greek text in order to make the passage read as if there are only three commandments that must be obeyed by Gentile converts. This, of course, is inconsistent with all other Scriptures and inaccurate. This particular subject is discussed in greater detail in the Walk in the Light Series book entitled *The Law and Grace*.

[21] The King James Version makes the same mistake.

[22] The correct Hebrew Name for the Messiah commonly called Jesus, is Yahushua. This subject is discussed in detail in the Walk in the Light Series book entitled *Names*.

[23] This is the same Psalms (Tehillim) quoted by Shaul in his letter to the Corinthians when he was dealing with meat sacrificed to idols. (1 Corinthians 10:26). Notice the duality of

the physical and the spiritual. "Clean hands" speaks of keeping our physical bodies clean while "pure heart" speaks of dealing with internal issues and being cleansed on the inside. Yahushua spent much of His earthly ministry teaching a people who understood the rule of purification concerning their bodies. His concern was that they understood the "big picture" and start getting cleaned up on the inside. He often rebuked the religious leaders who were so caught up on the external things that they missed the more important internal matters: the issues of the heart. Christianity, it seems, has gone to the other extreme. Christianity tries to spiritualize everything in the Scriptures but fails to realize that there are still practical issues of physical purity that must be learned and lived that also assist in our spiritual walk. There are both physical and spiritual dimensions to the Scriptures and you cannot ignore this fact without getting into trouble. Yahushua aptly demonstrated this fact in His teachings. He once said: "[27] *You have heard that it was said, 'Do not commit adultery.'* [28] *But I tell you that anyone who looks at a woman lustfully has already committed adultery with her in his heart.*" Mattityahu 5:27-28. Adultery was prohibited in the Torah and still is prohibited by the Torah. Not only are we supposed to keep our bodies from committing adultery, but also our hearts. You cannot truly live for Elohim if you believe that the Torah is old, irrelevant or superseded. The Torah is just as applicable today as it was in the days of Yahushua and Mosheh.

[24] John 1:1

[25] Adam Clarke's Commentary, Electronic Database, Copyright (c) 1996.

[26] The proper transliteration for the name of Apostle Paul is Shaul (sha ool).

[27] *The Scriptures*, The Institute for Scripture Research 1998.

[28] Mattithyahu 26:26.

[29] I refer to Yahushua using a form of the Hebrew word "moshiach" (מֹשִׁיחַ) that is translated Messiah and means "anointed". When you refer to Yahushua as The Messiah, there is no question what you mean, especially in the context of the Hebrew Scriptures. The word "christ" is a Greek term that also means "anointed," but is applied to any number of

their pagan gods. Therefore, the title Messiah is more appropriate when referring to the Hebrew Deliverer.

[30] Despite many attempts by secular and religious scholars to prove that Shaul started a new religion, there is not one shred of evidence that suggests he ever violated or advocated the abolition of the Torah. This was a lie which was spread about him when he was alive and it continues to this day. That was the primary reason why Yaakob encouraged Shaul to pay for others to fulfill their Nazarite vows. (see Acts 21:20-26; Bemidbar 6:1-21). By doing so he was demonstrating that not only did he observe the Torah, but he also taught and assisted others in their Torah observance.

[31] Kepha is the proper transliteration for the name of the disciple commonly called Peter.

[32] Adam Clarke's Commentary, Electronic Database. Copyright (c) 1996 (Elohim and Yahudim inserted by author).

[33] *The Jewish Roots of Acts*, LeCornu, Hilary and Shulam, Joesph, Acedom Printing 2003 Vol. I Page 562.

[34] This method of computation is called gematria and holds many insights for the student of Scripture as opposed to numerology, which is the perverted use of numbers used in witchcraft and sorcery.

[35] *The Origins of Christianity and the Bible*, The cultural background of early Christianity, www.religious-studies.info.

[36] *Dead Meat*, Sue Coe, Four Walls Eight Windows, 1995: Page 75.

[37] *Natural Cures "They" Don't Want You To Know About*, Kevin Trudeau, Alliance Publishing Group, Inc. 2004, Page 129.

[38] *What the Bible Says About Healthy Living*, Russel, Rex, M.D., Regal Books 1996, Page 154.

[39] Ibid at 154 citing *"It had to Happen, Scientist Examines Ancient Bathrooms of Romans 586 B.C."* Jane Cahill and Peter Warnock, Biblical Archaeological Review (May/June 1991) Pages 64-69.

[40] Ibid at 157 quoting *"Is your Seafood Safe?"* J. Pekkanen, Reader's Digest (July 1995) Page 122.

[41] This is particularly true concerning veal calf, which are kept in "veal sheds" also known as "crates." These crates are barely large enough to contain the growing calf that is unable to even turn around. The crates, typically 22 inches by 54 inches, are

intended to keep the muscles from growing to keep the flesh tender. In their miserable 14 week lifespan before they are slaughtered, the calves become anemic and suffer from open sores caused by rubbing against the crates. Also, chickens are treated terribly in hatcheries. "Inside the hatchery, each chicken is confined to about 48 to 86 square inches of space and these cages are piled tier upon tier. Due to severe overcrowding, layer hens are kept in semi-darkness. The stressed birds are de-beaked using hot irons (without anesthesia) to prevent them from pecking each other to death. The wire cages rub off their feathers, and the mesh floor cripples their feet." *Why Vegan* pamphlet, published by www.veganoutreach.org. "Today's chickens are allowed no expression of their natural urges. They cannot walk around, scratch the ground, build a nest, or even stretch their wings. Every instinct is frustrated." *Diet for a New America*, Robbins, John, Stillpoint, 1987:60.

[42] *Unholy Slaughter*, The International Jerusalem Post, No. 2301, December 10, 2004, 27 Kislev 5765, Page 7.

[43] One such account was provided by Dr. Temple Grandin and related by Ben Wolfson in his article entitled *Kosher Slaughter* Mishpahah Vol. 364, August 30, 1998, Pages 16-17. "She told me that the first time she visited a kosher slaughter house, she heard screaming cattle from a half kilometer away and wondered what was different in this place. What she saw was shocking. I quote from her book, *Thinking in Pictures, and Other Reports From My Life With Autism*: 'I will never forget having nightmares after visiting the now defunct Spencer Foods plant in Spencer, Iowa fifteen years ago. Employees wearing football helmets attached a nose tong to the nose of a writhing beast suspended by a chain wrapped around one back leg. Each terrified animal was forced with an electric prod to run into a small stall which had a slick floor on a forty-five degree angle. This caused the animal to slip and fall so that the workers could attach a chain to its rear leg [in order to raise it in the air]. As I watched this nightmare, I thought, 'This should not be happening in a civilized society'. In my diary I wrote, 'If hell exists, I am in it'. I vowed that I would replace the plant from hell with a kinder and gentler system.' And she has been

doing that for years now." Thankfully, the slaughterhouse described in her book is no longer operating but there may be other plants which still claim to be kosher and use inhumane methods to move and kill animals. The hope is that all kosher slaughter houses continue to improve so that they provide meat which is truly fit to consume and not actually treifa with a kosher symbol stamped upon the package. This hope is reassured by information which seems to indicate that certain kosher slaughter houses are taking significant measures to assure that their practices are humans. (See *Setting the Record Straight on Kosher Slaughter* by Menachem Genack Published February 15, 2005 The Commentator www.yucommentator.com).

[44] Leviticus (Vayiqra) 11:3.

[45] www.cnn.com/2004/HEALTH/01/08/salmon.pollution.ap/

[46] *What the Bible Says About Healthy Living*, Rex Russel, M.D., Regal Books 1996, Page 155 citing Chriastoph Scholtissek, M.D., *"Cultivating a Killer Virus."* National History (January 1992) Pages 302-307.

[47] Richard Harris, NPR, October 14, 2003.

[48] The word "church" is a man-made word typically associated with the Catholic and Christian religions. In that context it is usually meant to describe the corporate body of faith. It is used in most modern English Bibles as a translation for the Greek word "ekklesia" (εκκλησια) that simply means the "called out assembly of YHWH." The word "church" derives from pagan origins and its misuse is part of the problem associated with Replacement Theology which teaches that the "Church" has replaced Israel (Yisrael), which in Hebrew is called the "qahal" (קהל): "the called out assembly of YHWH." The Hebrew "qahal" and the Greek "ekklesia" are the same thing: The Commonwealth of Yisrael. Therefore, the continued use of the word "church" is divisive and confusing. This subject is described in grated detail in The Walk in the Light Series book entitled *The Redeemed.*

[49] This subject is discussed in greater detail in the Walk in the Light Series book entitled *Appointed Times.* Briefly, the Appointed Times of YHWH are detailed in Vayiqra Chapter 23 and include: the Sabbath, Passover, Unleavened Bread,

Shabuot, Yom Teruah, Yom Kippur, Sukkot and Shemini Atzeret. The Christian religion does not celebrate these Appointed Times even though YHWH clearly states that they are: "*My Appointed Times.*" (Vayiqra 23:2). Instead Christians celebrate Christmas and Easter, which both have significant and disturbing pagan roots and neither has any Scriptural basis. The tradition of incorporating pagan holidays into mainstream religion is discussed further in the Walk in the Light series book entitled *Pagan Holidays*.

50 The Names of the Father and Son are discussed in detail in the Walk in the Light Series book entitled *Names*.

51 See Matthew 8:11-12 and Luke 13:24-27. In both of these parables the Messiah speaks of a feast where the wicked are kicked out. The wicked and the lawless are treated the same – they are those who disobey the commandments.

52 *What the Bible Says About Healthy Living*, ibid at 150-161.

Appendix A

Clean Foods and Prohibited Items

These lists are meant to be a guide to assist in selecting some common kosher foods and are not be exhaustive.

Birds	Cattle	Insects
Chicken	Deer	Locust
Dove	Hart	Crickets
Duck	Sheep	Grasshoppers
Goose	Elk	
Grouse	Ibex	
Guinea	Antelope	
Partridge	Gazelle	
Peacock	Moose	
Pheasant	Giraffe	
Pigeon	Reindeer	
Song birds	Caribou	
Sparrow	Goat	
Quail		
Turkey		

Kosher Fish - Fish with fins and scales

Albacore	Amberjack
Anchovies	Angelfishes
Atlantic Pomfret	Atlantic Salmon
Ballyhoo	Barracudas
Bass	Bigeyes
Blackfish	Blacksmith
Blueback	Bluefish
Bluegill	Bonefish

Bonito	Bowfin
Bream	Brill
Buffalo fishes	Burbot
ButterFishes	Butterfly fish
Cabrilla	Calico bass
Capelin	Carps and minnows
Carosucker	Cero
Channel bass	Chilipepper
Chinook salmon	Chup
Cigarfish	Cisco
Coalfish	Cobia
Codfishes	Coho salmon
Corbina	Cottonwick
Crapplie	Creville
Croacker	Crucian carp
Cubbyu	Cunner
Damselfishes	Doctorfish
Dolly Varden	Dolphinfish
Drums	Flounders
Fluke	Flyingfishes
Frostfish	Gag See
Garibaldi	Giant kelpfish
Goatfishes	Gobies
Goldeye	Goldfish
Grayling	Graysby
Greenlings	Grindle
Grouper	Grunion
Grunts	Guavina
Haddock	Hakes
Halfbeak	Halfmoon
Halibut	Hamlet
Hardhead	Harvestfish
Hawkfishes	Herrings
Jack Mankerel	Jacks
Jacksmelt	Jewfish
KelpSish	Kingfish
Lafayette	Lake Herring
Lance	Largemouth bass

Lawyer
Lingcod
Lookdown
Mahimahi
Menpachii
Milkfish
Mooneye
Mouthbrooder
Muskellunge
Needlefishes
Palometa
Perches
Pickerel
Pikes
Pilchard
Plaice
Pomfret
Porgies
Poutassou
Quillback
Ray's bream
Roach
Rockfish
Rudderfish
Salmon
Sardine
Sauger
Scamp
Scorpionfishes
Sea bream
Seaperch
Seatrout
Sheepshead
Smallmouth bass
Snapper blue
Soles
Spanish mackerel
Splitttail

Leatherback
Lizardfishes
Mackerels
Margate
Merluccio
Mojarras
Mossbunker
Mullets
Muttonfish
Opaleye
Parrotfishs
Permit
Pigfish
Pikeperch
Pinfish
Pollock
Pompano
Porkfish
Queenfish
Rabalo
Red snapper
Rockhind
Rosefish
Runner Sablefish
Sand lances
Sargo
Scad
Schoolmaster
Sea bass
Sea chubs
Searobins
Shad
Silversides
Smelts
Snappers
Spadefishes
Spearing
Squawfish

Squirrelfishes
Striped bass
Surgeonfishes
Tench
Threadfins
Tilefishes
Tomtate
Tripletail
Tuna
Wahoo
Warmouth
WhiteFish
Wrasses
Yellowtail snapper

Steelhead
Surfperches
Tarpon
Tenpounder
Tilapia
Tomcod
Tomsmelt
Trout
Unicornfish
Walleye
Weakfishes
Whiting
Yellowtail

* Caviar is kosher if it comes from a kosher fish

Non Kosher Fish – Fish that do not have both fins and scales

Angler
Billfish
Bullhead
Catfish
Dogfish
Gars
Grayfish
Leatherjacket
Marlin
Ocean Pout
Paddlefish
Puffers
Ray
Rock Prickleback
Sculpins
Sharks
Skates
Snake Mackerels

Beluga
Blow Fish
Cabezon
Cutlass Fish
Eels
Goosefishes
Lampreys
Lomosuckers
Midshipman
Oilfish
Pout
Ratfish
Rock eel
Sailfish
Searaven
Sawfishes
Snailfishes
Spoonbill cat

Sturgeons	Swordfish
Toadfishes	Triggerfishes
Trunkfishes	Wolf Fishes

Also beware of shark marketed as "Lemon Fish"

Although not considered fish per se, all "seafood" that falls under the general category of shellfish is unclean and should not be eaten. The following is a list of some popular "seafood" items that are prohibited:

Clams	Crab
Lobster	Mussels
Octopus	Oysters
Prawn	Scallops
Shrimp	Squid (Calamari)

Appendix B

Resources

The resources listed herein are meant only to assist the reader in their quest for further information concerning kashrut, kosher foods and kosher related products. The sources may reflect a variety of opinions and perspectives which the author does not necessarily endorse and the reader is urged to use caution.

What the Bible Says About Healthy Living, Rex Russell, M.D., Regal Books 1996.

The Genesis Diet, Gordon S. Tessler, PhD., Be Well Publications, 1996

www.kashrut.com

www.kosher.co.il

www.okkosher.com

www.mykoshermarket.com

www.empirekosher.com

www.aaronsgourmet.com

www.kohnskosher.com

The internet is a valuable tool and can be used to find seemingly endless materials, references and stores which deal with this subject. This list is by no means exhaustive and is only a sampling of the resources which exist.

Appendix C

The Walk in the Light Series

Book 1   Restoration – A discussion of the pagan influences that have mixed with the true faith through the ages which has resulted in the need for restoration. This book also examines true Scriptural restoration.

Book 2   Names – Discusses the True Name of the Creator and the Messiah as well as the significance of names in the Scriptures.

Book 3   Scriptures – Discusses the origin of the written Scriptures as well as many translation errors which have led to false doctrines in some mainline religions.

Book 4   Covenants – Discusses the progressive covenants between the Creator and His Creation as described in the Scriptures which reveals His plan for mankind.

Book 5   The Messiah – Discusses the prophetic promises and fulfillments of the Messiah and the True identity of the Redeemer of Yisra'el.

Book 6   The Redeemed – Discusses the relationship between Christianity and Judaism and details how the Scriptures identify True Believers. It reveals how the Christian doctrine of Replacement Theology has caused confusion as to how the Creator views the Children of Yisra'el.

Book 7   The Law and Grace – Discusses in depth the false doctrine that Grace has done away with the Law and demonstrates the vital importance of obeying the commandments.

Book 8   The Sabbath – Discusses the importance of the Seventh Day Sabbath as well as the origins of the tradition concerning Sunday worship.

Book 9   Kosher – Discusses the importance of eating food prescribed by the Scriptures as a aspect of righteous living.

Book 10   Appointed Times – Discusses the appointed times established by the Creator, often erroneously considered to be "Jewish" holidays, and critical to the understanding of prophetic fulfillment of the Scriptural promises.

Book 11   Pagan Holidays – Discusses the pagan origins of some popular Christian holidays which have replaced the Appointed Times.

Book 12   The Final Shofar – Discusses the walk required by the Scriptures and prepares the Believer for the deceptions coming in the End of Days.

The series began as a simple Powerpoint presentation which was intended to develop into a book with twelve different chapters but ended up being twelve different books. Each book is intended to stand alone although the series was originally intended to build from one section to another. Due to the urgency of certain topics, the books have not been published in sequential order.

For announcements and additional teachings go to:

www.shemayisrael.net

Appendix D

The Shema
Deuteronomy (Debarim) 6:4-5

Traditional English Translation

Hear, O Israel: The LORD our God, the LORD is one!
You shall love the LORD your God with all your heart, with all
your soul, and with all your strength.

Corrected English Translation

Hear, O Yisrael: YHWH our Elohim, YHWH is one (unified)!
You shall love YHWH your Elohim with all your heart, with
all your soul, and with all your strength.

Modern Hebrew Text

שְׁמַע ישראל יהוה אלהינו יהוה אחד
ואהבת את יהוה אלהיך בכל־ לבבך ובכל־ נפשך ובכל־ מאדך

Ancient Hebrew Text

𐤀𐤇𐤃 𐤄𐤅𐤄𐤉 𐤅𐤍𐤉𐤄𐤋𐤀 𐤄𐤅𐤄𐤉 𐤋𐤀𐤓𐤔𐤉 𐤏𐤌𐤔
𐤊𐤁𐤁𐤋 𐤇𐤔𐤐𐤍 𐤋𐤊𐤁 𐤇𐤉𐤄𐤋𐤀 𐤄𐤅𐤄𐤉 𐤕𐤀 𐤕𐤁𐤄𐤀𐤅
𐤇𐤃𐤀𐤌 𐤋𐤊𐤁𐤅 𐤇𐤔𐤐𐤍

Hebrew Text Transliterated

Shema, Yisra'el: YHWH Elohenu, YHWH echad!
V-ahavta et YHWH Elohecha b-chol l'vavcha u-b-chol
naf'sh'cha u-b-chol m'odecha.

The Shema has traditionally been one of the most important prayers in
Judaism and has been declared the first (resheet) of all the Commandments.
(Mark 12:29-30).

Appendix E

Check the Ingredients

Many people mistakenly believe that cheese is dairy and therefore no possibility of not being kosher. Sadly, this is untrue. Enzymes are used in the cheese making process just as yeast is used to make beer.

There are a variety of enzymes that derive from different sources. Therefore, it is important to understand just what enzymes were used in the process when the cheese was produced. Some are derived from animals while others derive from plants and bacteria.

Rennet derives from the 4th stomach of a calf. Lipase is derived from calves, kids and lambs. Protease is derived from bovine (cow) glands Pancreatin and Trypsin come from desiccated pancreatic tissue, generally from swine.

Papain, Bromelain, Ficin and Amylase are the major plant-derived protease enzymes used commercially today. Microbial enzymes derived from the growth of microorganisms (bacteria, fungi and yeast) on nutrients through fermentation. Microbial rennet is used to make kosher cheese. (Note that rennet is not always considered to be halachically kosher unless the calf was killed in a kosher fashion)

I recommend looking for kosher symbols on cheeses or calling the company when there is a question regarding the source of enzymes.

Another problem ingredient found in many foods is gelatin. Gelatin is a product generally derived from animal skin, bones and tendons. Much of the gelatin produced in the United States comes from pigskins or cattle bones. There is vegetarian gelatin is available such as Agar-agar, which is derived from seaweed.

It pays to look at the ingredients.